MW01675766

Speaking to Communicate

An Introduction to Speech

Speaking to Communicate

An Introduction to Speech

Raymond L. Fischer
University of North Dakota

Waveland Press, Inc.
Prospect Heights, Illinois

For information about this book, write or call:

Waveland Press, Inc.
P.O. Box 400
Prospect Heights, Illinois 60070
(312) 634-0081

Copyright © 1972 by Raymond L. Fischer
1981 reissued by Waveland Press, Inc. Second printing.

ISBN 0-917974-77-8

All rights reserved. No part of this book may be reproduced, stored in a retrieval system, or transmitted in any form or by any means without permission in writing from the publisher.

Printed in the United States of America.

Contents

Preface

The title *Speaking to Communicate: An Introduction to Speech* implies that all speaking communicates what the speaker wishes to convey. Unfortunately, it does not. Often the words we use, the way we look, and the way we speak convey many meanings to our listeners—but not the meaning we are hoping for. In days of conflict and misunderstanding, it is extremely important that we say exactly what we intend to say in the way we wish to say it and that our listeners know exactly what we mean. This is an introduction to speech, a book for a first course in speaking. Its purpose is to assist you in preparing a speech correctly and in delivering it effectively.

Speaking actually consists of two procedures, preparation and delivery. The first three chapters are concerned with the proper preparation of a speech. Chapters four and five are concerned with the effective delivery of a speech. These five chapters can be applied to any speaking situation, in class or outside of class. The last four chapters of the book suggest speaking situations to which the fundamentals may be applied. The chapter on listening is included to assist you as a speaker and as a listener.

Although this book is written to assist you in writing and delivering speeches in class, much of the information is also directed to speeches to be given beyond the classroom. Since adults frequently are required to speak to an audience, the basic information given here should continue to assist you beyond your college career. In class or beyond the classroom, I hope that you learn to enjoy speaking, because the ability to write and deliver an effective speech is a rewarding experience.

Raymond L. Fischer

chapter one

CHOOSING A SUBJECT

Every step in preparing a speech must be carefully planned in advance. The first and most obvious step is choosing a subject. Before you can do anything else, you must decide upon a subject. Speakers often make choosing a subject much more difficult than it really is. If you keep in mind the following suggestions, choosing a subject should be easy.

I. GENERAL PURPOSE

Speaking consists of preparing and delivering original material or delivering the works of others. To write an original speech, you must first consider the general purpose of your speech. For the sake of convenience, all speeches can be categorized under three general purposes: speeches given *to inform*, to present unbiased information in order to increase the listener's knowledge about a subject; speeches *to entertain*, to create pleasurable diversion; and speeches *to persuade*, to attempt to influence the beliefs or actions of others.

Although one of the general purposes of a speech should always be dominant, the other general purposes are often subsidiary. Thus, when a speaker's purpose is to persuade, he may also inform or entertain, or both. The same is true with the other general purposes. In most cases, your instructor will state the general purpose of each speech assignment.

II. SPECIFIC PURPOSE

When you know what the general purpose of your speaking assignment is—that is, when you know that you are expected to give an informative speech to instruct, or an entertaining after-dinner speech, or a persuasive speech to convince—you might very well ask, "About what?" In other words, you still need to determine the specific purpose of your speech. As you consider different subjects, keep in mind the following suggestions.

A. Keep Yourself in Mind

Any specific purpose that you select should be interesting to you and should be something about which you have at least some knowledge. Too many students begin the job of selecting a specific purpose by going to the library to try to find an article from which they can report. Your first step should be to sit down and ask yourself, "What have I read or heard or seen that disturbs me?" Make a list of subjects that have caused you to stop and think or that have caused you to ask questions. Subjects on your list should be those to which you can easily relate, subjects that are relevant to *you*. Remember that you always communicate best what you are most interested in.

1. Consider Current Events. Is there a pressing problem on your campus, in your home town, or in your state that you would like to talk about? Are you especially concerned about national problems or problems that affect the entire world? Are you interested in getting something changed, in presenting a new view, in informing the class about your opinion?

Students are often concerned about housing, food, hours, grades, class, teachers, the administration, and other students. Do you agree with the way everything is handled on your campus? Are you active in any campus organizations? Do you disagree with the activities of radical or conservative campus groups? Perhaps you would like to inform, entertain, or persuade your listeners about what is actually happening, to give them the "real" story.

Possibly there is something happening in your home town or in your state that you would like to see changed—something to do with conservation, urban renewal, or unemployment. Maybe you would like to enlist the aid of fellow students to help you correct a bad situation. Are you aware of the issues being debated at home? Are you personally concerned with any of the issues?

Many national issues lend themselves to good speeches. All of us are naturally interested in peace, although we may disagree about the means of securing peace. Everyone is concerned with pollution, drug usage, welfare, human rights, space exploration. Is there one issue that means more to you than any other? Do you agree or disagree with what is being done about the issue in Washington?

2. *Consider Travel.* Have you been to interesting places, seen interesting things? Possibly you have observed or taken part in some of the history-making events at the state or national level. A first-hand account is always interesting. You may want to persuade your audience that a previous report of an event did not include all of the facts or both sides.

3. *Consider Work.* Many students work part time or full time while they attend school; others may have interesting summer employment. Is there something about your work that is unusual, something that you particularly like or dislike, something that you would like to see changed? Perhaps you have had humorous experiences while at work. Possibly your work has encouraged or discouraged your studies in certain areas.

4. *Consider Classes.* Your classroom work is probably interesting to you. Your major or minor fields may supply you with subject material. Are you learning something unusual? Do any of your classes provide startling experiences? Are you preparing for an interesting occupation or profession? Would you suggest that other students change their majors? Are you learning anything in class that will assist you in solving any of the problems around you?

5. *Consider Literature.* Do you like to read? Reading opens up literally thousands of topics for a speech. Perhaps you like to read histories, biographies, accounts of travel, or scientific works. Possibly you like mysteries or science fiction. Do you have a favorite author? Reading may suggest subjects about which you would like to learn more. Do not try to give book reports; rather, let your reading be a guide to more information. For example, a speech about ecology should not be based on just one author's viewpoint. If you have been stimulated by an ecology text, use your interest as a beginning point: explore local situations, read other works about ecology, or consult with experts in the field.

6. *Consider Hobbies, Sports, Musical Instruments, Games.* Your favorite pastime may provide you with information for a speech. Do you collect anything? Items that you have been putting back in a box or a drawer—mementos or souvenirs from trips, dances, or other important events in your life—may very well provide you with a subject. You may have a hobby and may not even know it.

Most students either participate in one or more sports or follow sports events as observers. You do not have to play baseball to give an interesting speech about it. As a matter of fact, people who watch a game may know as much or more about the sport as someone who participates in it; a spectator at a football game has a vantage point better than that of the player on the field. If you participate in sports or just watch sports, the chances are good that you could give an interesting speech about athletics. Remember, the sport does not have to be one that is attended by thousands of people. Ping pong or handball can be the subject of an interesting speech.

Do you play a musical instrument? Many people take piano lessons and many play musical instruments for fun in the privacy of their own rooms. Such an interest in music may be just a pastime for you, but it may make an interesting speech. You might, for instance, compare different types of music, explain how an instrument works or how it was developed, or persuade someone to learn to play an instrument.

Do you have a favorite game that you like to play? Do you like to play bridge, poker, or other card games? Do you pass the time with chess or checkers? Is there a game that you are interested in that others may not be familiar with? Such an interest could become the basis for a speech.

B. Keep Your Audience in Mind

Not only should the subject you select be relevant to you; it should also be relevant to your audience. Try to determine as clearly as possible what would be interesting to your audience. Considering certain factors about your audience may help you choose a subject.

1. Consider Knowledge. Do most of those in your audience know as much about your subject as you do? If so, they probably would not be interested in what you have to say. If your subject is one about which a great deal is known, you may want to take a different or an unusual approach to the subject, or you may want to add a new "twist" to the topic. Above all, try to pick a subject that is current, pertinent, and relevant—one that will make your audience want to learn more.

2. Consider Composition. If possible, try to consider the composition of your audience. Will it be predominantly men or women; will it be children, young people, or adults? If your audience will be composed predominantly of people your own age, they will more than likely be interested in the things that interest you. If your audience will be composed of older people in a retirement village, or of Boy Scouts or Girl Scouts, you must take this into consideration. If your audience will be predominantly men your own age, they probably would not appreciate a speech concerning dressmaking; if predominantly women, you might avoid subjects such as changing spark plugs or the intricacies of a football play. On the other hand, almost any topic can be *made* interesting to any group. One student, keeping in mind that his audience was composed mainly of women, demonstrated how easily a tire can be changed, pointing out that there are times when a woman must change a tire herself.

3. Consider Background. Although it may be difficult to determine the background of an audience, you should try to learn about the audience's educational, social, political, and religious background. Many times an audience will have one or more background factors in common. The audience may be individuals having basically the same educational standing; that is, student teachers, graduate students, teachers, or administrators. If you are speaking to a group of highly educated individuals, you must take care to choose a subject appropriate to them. The same care must be taken if you are speaking to a group of less educated individuals. Many times speakers are accused of "talking over the heads" of an audience or "speaking down" to them. The social background of your audience should also be taken into consideration. Is your audience sophisticated or provincial? Finally, a speaker may consider the political or religious background of his audience. In certain parts of our country, religious groups and/or political parties predominate. This knowledge could very well help you select a topic; it might also help you avoid antagonizing a biased faction.

C. Other Considerations

The season of the year may give you some ideas for a speech. If your speech occurs during a season that includes special activities, you might consider one of these activities. Speeches given during a holiday season are often a part of a special occasion or celebration. In addition, the size of the audience or the conditions under which you are to speak might influence your choice of subject.

III. NARROWING THE SUBJECT

Once you have determined your general purpose (to inform, to entertain, or to persuade) and have chosen a specific purpose relevant both to you and to your audience, the next step is to narrow your subject. One of the most important things to remember in this respect is the time limit. How long do you have to speak? Most of your speeches in class will be less than ten minutes long. The time assigned may seem an eternity at first; but after you have gathered information and collected your thoughts, you will more than likely find that you have much more information than you can possibly use. Also consider that you could not adequately cover a subject like "pollution" in several hours, let alone ten minutes. The first step might be to decide upon a specific area within the subject; pollution of the air, or water, or land—any one of these—might make a more reasonable speech. Or you may find that these specific areas need to be limited even further—for instance, to one type of air pollution. Similarly, if you decide upon the topic of photography, you will find it necessary to narrow your topic. You might consider such areas as how to take pictures, or how to develop pictures, or how to enlarge pictures. More than likely such topics *could be* well covered in a short period of time. Remember, however, that you cannot perform all of the actual steps of developing a picture within a five-minute time limit. By explaining each of the different steps and then displaying a finished product, you can observe any time limitation.

When you narrow your subject, be certain that there is *enough* information available about that subject. A student desiring to persuade his audience that America's nuclear arsenal is superior to that of Russia might find that very little information is available concerning Russia's weapons and that what information is available is mainly speculative.

IV. STATING THE PURPOSE

Once you have selected a general purpose and a specific purpose and have narrowed your subject, you should state your purpose clearly. Such a statement will help you to determine for yourself whether you *have* a definite purpose to begin with. What do you hope to achieve by your speech? Your object should be written as a simple declarative sentence stating what you intend to do: "I am going to demonstrate to my audience how to take a picture," or "I am going to relate my experiences as a babysitter in order to entertain my audience," or "I am going to attempt to convince my audience that the United Nations should be strengthened by having a permanent military force." Your instructor may require you to include your purpose as part of your speech, either as a central point or as a statement of purpose. In any case, this is a necessary step before you start to gather information for your speech.

SUMMARY

The first step in preparing any speech is to choose a subject. The first step in choosing a subject is to know your general purpose: to inform, to entertain, or to persuade. When the general purpose is determined, you must select a specific purpose. The specific purpose must be something that is interesting and important to both you and your audience. The specific purpose may be selected from current events, your travel, your work, your classes, your reading, or your pastimes. You should keep in mind the knowledge, composition, and background of your audience, and other special considerations that might help you select a subject.

When you have selected a subject that will be interesting to you and your audience, narrow your subject. Be certain that you can adequately cover your subject in the time assigned and that there is sufficient information available.

Finally, word your subject in such a way that you know exactly what you want to accomplish. Write your purpose in a simple declarative statement.

ASSIGNMENTS

1. Look through last week's issues of a newspaper. Make a list of the headlines found on the front pages.
2. List the topics discussed in the last ten issues of *Current History* or *Congressional Digest.*
3. Select five topics discussed on radio or television "talk" shows.
4. Make a list of at least five things that you would like to see changed on your campus.
5. List in the order of importance ten issues that you consider most important in the world today.

chapter two

SPEECH CONTENT

When you have completed the first step in preparing a speech (that of selecting a topic, narrowing your topic, and carefully wording exactly what you want to accomplish), the second step is to gather the information that will help you to inform, entertain, or persuade.

One of the most profitable side effects of speech class is the accumulation of useful information. You will acquire information that will contribute not only to the interest and value of your speech but also to your conversation, your social activities, and your other classes.

I. SOURCES OF SPEECH CONTENT

Generally speaking, there are three major sources of information: personal knowledge, the library, and personal interviews. Radio and television, although entertaining, seldom can be considered good sources of information. A good rule of thumb is to remember that (with the exception of interviews) the information you use in your speeches should be available to everyone; in other words, it should be in written form. Unless you record the information as it is presented, you will seldom be able to get all of the details as the information is delivered via radio or television. Use these media as sources for subjects, not information.

A. Personal Knowledge

The first step in informing yourself about a subject is to recall what you already know about it. Write down what you have already learned about the subject you have chosen; you may be surprised to find that you are already aware of many relevant facts, examples, illustrations, and ideas. Your list will also serve as a valuable point of departure toward further research. One of the best things you can do is to put your ideas in the form of a "rough" outline, a listing of as many major points and subpoints as possible at this time (see Figure 1). Do not attempt to make a complete formal outline, for a "rough" outline will be sufficient to show where you must concentrate most of your time in gathering information. It will also help you plan your time at the library and further activities such as arranging an interview with someone who is an authority on your subject or planning a trip to a place where you can learn about the subject by means of observation and experience.

Thinking about your subject is an important part of writing a speech: you will have to think about the relative importance of the information that you gather and about changing your ideas as new information and ideas come to you. Thinking about your subject over a period of time helps to give your speech the element of originality that adds to the value placed on your words by others. Your speech should not remind listeners of articles that they have read. On the contrary, your words should exhibit the marks of individuality that have resulted from your personal experiences, reflection, and creative thinking.

B. The Library

The primary source of information for any speaking situation is the library. Reading is an exceedingly important factor in conversation, discussion, and in all other forms of speaking. The following suggestions have been found to develop mature reading: cultivate a genuine enthusiasm for reading, try to read at least a little every day, vary the material that you read, look for more than just the obvious meanings in what you read, critically analyze what you read, consider what you read in the light of what you already know, and, above all, adjust your reading to reflect your current need for information.

1. Books. Usually, the first source of information that a speaker refers to when he visits the library is books. You can find information in books upon virtually any subject in which you are interested. After you have decided upon a subject for a speech, you will probably find it helpful to look in the library card catalog or the *Cumulative Book Index* for help. The library card catalog contains the names of all the books in that library, and the *Cumulative Book Index* lists practically all books in print. If you wish to use books that the library does not have, you can many times obtain them from the nearest public library. Occasionally, you may want to ask a librarian to send to the state library or to another school for a book that you need.

There are a number of books called *indexes* that may prove useful to you. They contain detailed information about articles and books within specific fields. Among them are such indexes as *Agricultural Index*, *Art Index*, *Education Index*, and *Industrial Arts Index.*

There are many yearbooks to which you should go for information at times. Among these are *American Yearbook*, *Statesman's Yearbook*, *Who's Who in America*, *World Almanac*, and the *Statistical Abstract.* You will find it worthwhile to examine these books carefully to note the types of information that they contain.

As you set about informing yourself upon a subject, you will often find it necessary to consult encyclopedias. Among the standard encyclopedias are *Encyclopedia Americana*, *Encyclopaedia Britannica*, and *The New International Encyclopedia.* However, you should never rely entirely on an encyclopedia. Speeches written almost entirely from articles found in an encyclopedia lack depth and originality. Such speeches are obviously encyclopedic to the instructor and usually bore the audience.

If you have difficulty expressing a particular thought or feeling, you may be helped by a dictionary or an encyclopedia of quotations. Such books may contain appropriate, striking, and/or beautiful expressions of the thought you want to express. Quotations also can be valuable in getting the audience's attention in the introduction and in summarizing your ideas in the conclusion. Among the best books of quotations and their compilers are *Familiar Quotations* by John Bartlett, *Speaker's Encyclopedia* by Jacob M. Braude, *Every Man's Dictionary of Quotations and Proverbs* by David Clayton Browning, *Hoyt's New Cyclopedia of Practical Quotations* edited by Kate L. Roberts, *The Home Book of Quotations and Proverbs* by Burton Stevenson, and *The Home Book of Quotations*, also by Mr. Stevenson.

2. *Magazines.* Some magazines appear weekly, some biweekly, some monthly, and some quarterly. As a group, they contain a wider variety of material than that contained in books. When you are looking for material concerning a specific subject, you can most often locate it by consulting the *Readers' Guide to Periodical Literature.* This journal appears every two weeks and lists the articles that appear in most of the magazines of merit.

Among the many magazines that speech students find especially valuable are *Congressional Digest*, *Current History*, *Vital Speeches of the Day*, *Newsweek*, *Time*, *U.S. News & World Report*, *New Repub-*

General Purpose: To persuade
Specific Purpose: To persuade about smoking
Narrowing the Purpose: Smoking is detrimental.
Stating the Purpose: I will persuade my audience that they should stop smoking because it is detrimental.

Introduction: Personal experiences might help establish rapport with the audience. Doctor's statement about growing number of deaths from lung cancer or a statement about increase in lung diseases might get attention. A word picture comparing a healthy lung and a smoker's lung would probably get attention and give a general idea about my topic.

I. Smoking damages the mind
    A. Memory or retention is damaged
        1. Personal experiences before and after smoking
        2. Check with Dr. Johnson on this
        3. Check heart society pamphlet concerning nicotine and blood supply to the brain
    B. Logical thinking is impaired
        1. Look for research article from science class on this subject
        2. Mention what doctor said when dad went to see him about dizzy spells
        3. Check with friends who have stopped smoking

II. Smoking affects many parts of the body (keep lung disease till last, seems most impressive)
    A. Smoking affects the senses

1. Taste is affected by smoking
    a. Inability to distinguish tastes
        (1) Tongue feels fuzzy
        (2) Roof of mouth sore
        (3) Mention how good everything tastes when not smoking
    b. Locate article about number of taste buds affected by each cigarette
2. Smell is affected by smoking
    a. Smoke affects nose and therefore the sense of smell (and taste)
    b. Check articles on this
    c. See what Dr. Johnson says

B. Smoking affects the heart
1. Use brochure from the Heart Association
2. Mention doctor's recommendation that dad stop smoking because of heart
3. Check Readers' Guide

C. Smoking causes upper respiratory diseases
1. Several books in the library have articles about diseases other than cancer caused by smoking
2. Ask Dr. Johnson about new developments
3. Cancer caused by smoking
    a. Number of deaths
    b. Increased smoking means increase in cancer

Conclusion: Mention reasons for not smoking. Refer to figures mentioned in introduction and point out that of the twenty-five people in the room, three are doomed to die unless they stop smoking.

Figure 1. Rough Outline.

lic, *Harper's*, and *Atlantic*. There are many other magazines in your library that relate to your interests and for that reason are good sources for speech materials. A word of caution, however. Just as too many speakers first head for encyclopedias, too many use the *Reader's Digest* as the primary, if not the only, source of information. Remember that the *Reader's Digest* is just that, a digest. It should be used as a source for ideas and as a guide for additional material; it should be a means to material, not an end in itself.

3. Newspapers. A newspaper's chief value lies in the fact that it provides information about current events and conditions almost as soon as they happen. To be well informed you should read at least the local newspaper every day. Forming this habit will provide you with an abundance of current material for use in speaking. You should also try to read a newspaper that has achieved a national reputation—for instance, *The Christian Science Monitor* and *The New York Times. The New York Times Index* is extremely valuable for finding specific newspaper articles. *Facts on File* can also be helpful in locating material in newspapers.

Because newspapers are printed in haste, the information in them sometimes lacks proper proportion and is sometimes inaccurate. Furthermore, the facts in newspapers sometimes are selected to support the editorial policy of the newspaper. Magazines are more valuable as source material because they are more accurately and more carefully written. If critically read, however, a newspaper can be a valuable source of speech material.

4. The Librarians. Although working independently in the library should be your goal, do not overlook the importance of the librarians, who know the resources of the library better than anyone else. You may wish to ask them at times if they have materials in their files relating to the subject in which you are interested. On many subjects your library will have files containing clippings, pamphlets, and pictures. The librarians can also direct you to sources of information about which you are unaware.

C. Personal Interviews

A valuable source of information is an interview with a recognized, unbiased authority. Make use of the experience and knowledge of people on campus, in industry, and in the community. You are surrounded by men and women who have specialized in certain areas of knowledge: instructors have special training in their fields and they will be happy to share their knowledge; every town has its doctors, lawyers, nurses, church officials, and government officials, people who are usually willing to give their time to a student interested in their special fields. The important thing to remember is that an authority's time should never be wasted. If you decide to use the interview method of gathering information, plan your questions ahead of time and listen carefully when the answers are given. Following the interview you should send a thank-you note in which you explain how you used the interview information in your speech and how the information was received and accepted.

II. RECORDING SPEECH CONTENT

After you have recorded in a "rough" outline the mental inventory of the information you already know about your subject, you will discover additional ideas and information. This information should be inserted into the "rough" outline as soon as possible. New information will come from books and magazines, and if possible at least one authority should be interviewed as a source of information. You may find that as you work with a subject, your own ideas change.

As you gather information for your speech, record your findings. Information should be recorded accurately and immediately, for within a very short time we forget most of what we hear and a good deal of what we read. There are several ways to record material. A few of the best ways follow. The individual must discover for himself the way most efficient for him.

A. Note Cards

Note cards are especially convenient because they can be arranged according to the topics and subtopics to which they relate. They are also easily carried and thus conveniently available when needed. Files of various kinds are an aid in keeping and organizing the information on note cards. When you record information on note cards, keep in mind the following suggestions:

> Use cards of uniform size. Note cards can be obtained in several sizes; however, most speakers prefer 4″ x 6″ cards. These are large enough to record most information; yet they are a convenient size for handling.
>
> Use only one side of each card.
>
> Record only one idea or one quotation on each card. This will allow you to organize your materials within individual topics.
>
> Record only the most concise, important, and impressive statements that you can find concerning a specific subject.

Criminal use of the telephone I., A., 1.

John Jones, The Criminal (New York: Smith Publishing Company, 1969).

Organized crime uses the telephone more than any other method of communication. The phone is considered essential for gambling as well as for many other aspects of crime. When phones were removed from gambling establishments, their activities were severely curtailed. In many cities, such as New York, Chicago, . . . and St. Louis, the telephone was the only method used to place bets.

p. 42

Figure 2. Note Card Containing Source Information and Direct Quotation.

Any unimportant or unnecessary information should be omitted from within the quotations. Ellipses (. . .) should be used to show omissions. When an ellipsis comes at the end of a statement marked with a period, that period precedes the three dots.

Indicate with square brackets any explanatory comments that you insert within a quotation.

Before putting the card aside, check quotations carefully for errors that you might have made in wording, punctuation, or details.

Quotations should not be selected or taken out of context so that they misrepresent what the writer has said.

Write carefully and clearly or type the cards, so that the information can be easily read.

Two basic methods are used to record information on note cards. The first method (see Figure 2) is to place all of the information on one card.

The upper left corner of the card should contain a short description of the material found on the card. In the upper right corner, symbols are used to show where the card is to be used in the outline. These symbols should be in *pencil*, because the symbols will probably change as the final outline evolves. The source information can be placed on the card as shown above or at the bottom of the card. If placed at the bottom of the card, the source information should include the page number: John Jones, *The Criminal* (New York: Smith Publishing Company, 1969), p. 42. This information is in the form of a footnote. If you are instructed to document your speech, be certain to use a reputable guide such as *The MLA Style Sheet* or Kate I. Turabian's *A Manual for Writers of Term Papers, Theses and Dissertations.* Since proper form differs from guide to guide, choose one guide and use it consistently. Finally, note that a space is used between the short description and the source information and between the source information and the quotation.

The second method is to use two cards, one for the source information and another for any quotation or information taken from the source. This does not mean that only one quotation is to be used from each source. As many quotation cards as necessary should be used. This method saves the time of putting the source information on each quotation card and also allows more room for the quotation. (See Figures 3 and 4.)

John Jones I

The Criminal

New York

Smith Publishing Company

1969

Figure 3. Source Card.

The first "I" in the upper right corner of the quotation card is the source-identification symbol. This symbol is for identification only; it indicates that the quotation was taken from the source found on the source card with the same symbol. The symbols "I., A., 1." show

I

Criminal use of the telephone I., A., 1.

Organized crime uses the telephone more than any other method of communication. . . .

p. 42

Figure 4. Quotation Card.

where the quotation fits into the outline. When this form is used, the page number always appears on the quotation card.

Either method can also be used for magazines and newspapers. Again, check a reputable guide to be certain what information should appear in a footnote, for this is the same information that should be included on the source card. For an interview, the source card should include the name of the individual interviewed, that part of his title which indicates he is an authority, the date of the interview, and the location of the interview.

B. Notebook or Folders

Much of what has just been said about recording information on cards also applies to placing information in a looseleaf notebook or in a manila folder. The distinguishing aspect of this method is that each sheet of paper is headed with a topic from the outline and all information about the topic is placed on the same sheet of paper. Only one side of the paper should be used. (See Figure 5.)

C. Clipping

A third way to record information is to write down the information without a particular method of organization. As you record the information, leave several spaces between each entry. A short summary of the quotation should be placed above the quotation, and source information should follow the quotation. (See Figure 6.) When all of the needed information has been recorded, the quotations are cut apart. Using the major points of your outline as guides, place the quotations in stacks. Each stack, as a main point, can then be reorganized into smaller stacks, or subpoints.

III. ORGANIZING SPEECH CONTENT

After the material has been gathered, thought must be given to its organization. The most common form of organization is to divide the speech into three parts: the introduction, the body, and the conclusion. Each part of the speech is important in its own right, and each has several functions to perform.

A. The Introduction

The introduction is, of course, the first part of your speech. You may find, however, that it is better to wait to complete the introduction until after you have planned the body of the speech. On the other hand, a good introduction can direct your work in writing the body of the speech. Experience and practice will help you discover the method which is better for you.

Because the introduction is important, it should be carefully planned. An introduction should be long enough to include what is needed, but short enough to be easily followed. A long introduction can lose the audience and burden the speaker. Remember that because the introduction should be delivered as planned, it should be written out and in most cases memorized.

The introduction of any speech should perform three functions: it must get the audience's interest and attention, it must give a general idea of the purpose of the speech, and it must include a transition into the body of the speech.

1. Getting Audience's Interest and Attention. There are several ways to get the audience's interest and attention. A speaker might very well use one or a combination of the following ways.

a. Common Interests. A speaker can often gain interest and attention by citing something that he and his audience have in common. If he is speaking in a small town or a farm community, and he himself grew up in a small town or on a farm, he could profitably mention the similarity. If he is speaking to students, he can mention his own experiences in school. The speaker might say something

Smoking causes cancer

Cigarette smoking is causally related to lung cancer. . . . The risk of developing lung cancer increases with duration of smoking and the number of cigarettes smoked per day. . . . (U. S. Surgeon General's Report, January 1971, p. 8)

Twenty-five studies in ten countries have shown that the death rate from lung cancer in cigarette smokers is about ten times that of nonsmokers. It is estimated that about 75 per cent of lung cancer is caused by smoking. (Cigarette Smoking and Lung Cancer, American Cancer Society, 1971, p. 2)

Cigarette smokers' death rates from cancer of the upper respiratory tract (lip, tongue, mouth, pharynx, larynx, and esophagus) were seven times that of nonsmokers in a study of 185,000 men between ages 50 and 69. (Your Health and Cigarettes, American Cancer Society, 1970, p. 3)

Cigarette smoking is a significant factor in the causation of laryngeal cancer. . . . There is a direct relationship between smoking and cancers of the buccal cavity, pharynx, and esophagus. (Smoking, Tobacco, and Health, U. S. Department of Health, Education, and Welfare, 1969, p. 19)

The Surgeon General's Report concluded that evaluation of the evidence leads to the judgment that cigarette smoking is a significant factor in the causation of laryngeal cancer in the male, the causation of tobacco-esophageal cancer, cancer of the larynx, and cancer of the pharynx. (The Health Consequences of Smoking, U. S. Department of Health, Education, and Welfare, 1967, p. 148)

When a smoker takes a long drag on a cigarette, he pulls the smoke into the farthest recesses of the lungs. . . . In this process, the sticky tar with its many chemical constituents, including several cancer-causing agents, is deposited on the mucous membrane of the entire bronchial system. . . . The combined tar, chemicals (some cancer-causing agents), and gases irritate the mucous membrane. The tar continues to collect on the mucous membrane, and after a variable number of years the mucosal cells become altered. Many flatten and increase in number. The nuclei become larger, the cells heap up and then begin to grow inward. This produces a cancer in many individuals after a period of years. The cancer spreads into the surrounding lung structure and invades lymph and blood vessels. Groups of the cancer cells separate and are carried by the lymph and bloodstream to other parts of the body to develop into metastatic tumors. (If You Smoke–Here's What Your Doctor May See, Narcotics Education, Inc., P. O. Box 4390, Washington, D.C. 20012–price 10¢)

Figure 5. Information Recorded in Looseleaf Notebook.

Smoking

Symptoms of lung cancer

The symptoms of lung cancer are persistent cough, blood in the sputum, a lingering infection of the lung, or pain in the chest; but by the time these appear, the disease has usually progressed too far to be cured.

Cigarette Smoking and Lung Cancer, American Cancer Society, 1965, p. 3.

Smoking and death rate

The Surgeon General of the Public Health Service appointed a committee of 10 persons, experts whose names had been submitted to and approved by the tobacco industry, who spent over a year reviewing all the research up to that time [1969]. The committee found smoking is associated with a 70 percent increase in the age-specific death rates of males, which means that on the average, for every 10 deaths among men who do not smoke, there will be 17 deaths among an equal number of men of the same age who do.

Smoking, Tobacco, and Health, U. S. Department of Health, Education, and Welfare, 1969, p. 8.

Smoking and fires

Last year there were 163,900 fires linked to smoking or the matches used in smoking, with a concomitant property loss of $80,400,000. . . . The statistics on the number of deaths attributed to those fires are not available, but it is estimated that 1,800 people per year will die due to fires caused by smoking and matches.

The Health Consequences of Smoking, U. S. Department of Health, Education, and Welfare, 1970, p. 188.

Figure 6. The "Clipping" Method of Recording Information.

appreciative about the town, the building in which he is speaking, or the audience. The comments should be sincere; avoid such trite phrases as "It is nice to see such happy smiling faces," "It is good to be here tonight," and "What a nice place you have here." Do not say something about the classroom situation in which you find yourself when you are giving a speech for speech class.

b. Word Picture. One of the best ways to get interest and attention is to start with a word picture or description. If you are talking about juvenile crime, you might describe a specific holdup or give a narrative description of a young person shoplifting. If your topic concerns pollution, a description of a beautiful river before and after pollution might be very effective. If you are concerned about hunger, you might very well describe a starving child with its pitifully distended stomach, its sores, its crying. It is not necessary that the word picture or description be factual; however, caution should be used to avoid both overdramatization and descriptions that are repulsively lurid. In addition, care should be taken not to use such trite phrases as "Picture if you will . . ." or "Return with me to the scene. . . ."

c. Rhetorical Questions. Another way to get the interest and attention of the audience is to ask rhetorical questions—questions to which answers are not expected. "Did you ever wonder what a man thinks about just before he dies?" (in reference to capital punishment) or "Will you be thinking about a baby dying of starvation as you sit down to your evening meal?" Such overused expressions as "Are you aware that . . .?" or "Did you know that . . .?" should be avoided.

d. Startling Facts and Statistics. Unusual or little-known facts and figures, particularly those presented in an interesting manner, are likely to get an audience's interest and attention. For example, rather than just stating that a baby is born every ten seconds, you might start with "Ten, nine, eight, seven, six, five, four, three, two, one, zero. The countdown for a nuclear explosion? No, the countdown for a population explosion. Every ten seconds a new baby is born; every ten seconds there is a new mouth to be fed."

Never use facts or figures just as a device to get attention. The facts and figures used should be about your topic and should help your audience understand your topic. A convention speaker once introduced his speech by citing several little-known facts and figures. He then stated that since he had gained everyone's attention he would go on with what he really wanted to talk about. He soon lost the attention of most of his audience.

e. Humor. The use of a humorous story or an anecdote often serves to get interest and attention. However, it should be kept in mind that humor is not applicable to all speeches and that humor has a tendency to detract from the more serious object of the speech. An audience may think about a humorous story that has been told or wait for the next story rather than listen to any serious thought that you may be presenting. If used, humor should be used sparingly unless the purpose of the speech is to entertain. The best humor that can be used is a humorous incident that has happened to the speaker; this type of humor is more believable and also helps to establish rapport.

f. Quotation or Poetry. A pertinent quotation or a short poem can often be used to gain attention in the introduction. Several sources for this type of material have already been mentioned. It should be remembered that a *short* quotation or a *few* lines of poetry will usually suffice. Naturally, the quotation or poetry should have something to do with your topic. One of the best sources for quotations and poetry is an anthology of works with which you are familiar. You must appreciate the quotation, for you must be sincere if you are to be effective.

2. *Relating the Purpose.* In addition to getting interest and attention, the introduction should relate the purpose of the speech. The audience should never have to guess what your purpose for speaking is. You might try to find an original way to state your purpose: "There is really only *one* way an *Italian* would make a pizza" or "There is a growing list of rationalizations about our failure to wear seat belts; there is also a growing list of traffic fatalities." Or you might feel more secure if you use a specific statement of purpose. Either way, the audience should know what you intend to do.

3. *Transition.* Finally, the introduction should include a transition into the body of the speech. This transition should be a statement that puts the speech in its proper perspective, that tells the audience the introduction is over and you are ready to pursue the main ideas of your speech. You might use a rhetorical question as a transition: "What are the students of America doing about this problem?" or a simple statement: "Let us see what is really causing the situation." The statement of purpose might also be part of the transition. The transition should lead the audience gently but obviously into the body of the speech.

B. The Body

Because the message is presented in the body of the speech, this portion of the speech should be outlined; in fact, organization is the most important aspect of the body of the speech. The theme suggested in the introduction should be developed carefully, and the steps and ideas should follow some obvious pattern. Ideally, the speaker should work from an outline which should be easy for his audience to follow.

1. Speech Patterns. Whatever your purpose, a definite pattern must be followed. A pattern is a point-by-point development of the purpose. To be able to communicate properly with your audience, you must present them with a pattern that can be easily followed. Each point must logically lead to the following point, and all points should be concerned with the purpose. There are several patterns that can be used.

a. Chronological Pattern. One of the most often used patterns is the time pattern. If your purpose is to inform your audience of the life of a well-known individual, you would more than likely begin with his early life, follow this with information about his youth, then discuss his adult life, and conclude with his old age. If you are explaining the making of bread, you might start with the planting of the wheat followed by the harvesting, grinding, mixing, baking, wrapping, and delivering. If you want to inform your audience about hunger, you might progress from the early pains to the later pains, the distortion of the body, and finally the lethargy. The pattern is one that is easily followed and easily remembered.

b. Spatial Pattern. If your purpose is descriptive, you may find the spatial pattern useful. If you were to describe the Library of Congress, you might describe the way in which each room leads from the main reading room after describing the main reading room itself. If your purpose is to educate, you might use the spatial pattern to inform your audience about the inside of a space capsule.

c. Step-by Step Pattern. If your purpose is to give a demonstration, you could very well use the step-by-step pattern. If you are demonstrating how to make a cake, you might point out that the first step is to make certain that you have all of the ingredients on hand. This is followed by the second step, mixing the shortening and sugar, then adding the eggs, followed by flour and milk, and so on until the cake is finished. Each step must take place in the correct order or the cake will be a failure. All speeches to demonstrate use a pattern of steps in a particular order.

d. Topical Pattern. Many speeches which do not fall under any other type of pattern use topics as a pattern in themselves. If you are speaking about modes of transportation, your topics could be land, sea, and air. If you are informing your audience about weapons, your topics might be hand weapons, shoulder weapons, and field pieces.

e. Problem-Solution, Need-Plan, Question-Answer Patterns. If your purpose is to persuade, one of these similar patterns might be followed. Although these patterns usually include only two main headings, you may wish to add a third heading, such as "Benefits," "Feasibility," "Results," or "Applications." These patterns can also be used for a speech to inform. In such a speech, the first point could be devoted to analyzing the problem, need, or question; and the second point to showing why the solution, plan, or answer is the best.

f. Cause and Effect or Effect and Cause Pattern. Here again, the speech would include only two main points. Your purpose could be either to inform or to persuade.

g. Past, Present, Future Patterns. This pattern is most often used with a speech to inform but could also be used with a speech to persuade. With this pattern, the speaker first examines the events of the past and discusses their relationship to the present situation. He then describes the present situation, and finally he projects his ideas concerning the future.

Each major point of any pattern must be presented in such a way that the audience can easily understand that point and its relationship to all others. Each point should be summarized before the next point is taken up. A simple transition such as "And now, let us look at the next point" or "The next step consists of . . ." should be included between major points.

2. Outlining. The ability to outline effectively is a key to good thinking, good writing, and good speaking. If you develop this ability, it will almost certainly improve your work in every subject that you study. An outline is called many things—a map, a blueprint, a foundation, a skeleton; but it is actually none of these. It is a *condensation* of the body of your speech arranged and worded in such a way that it is easy for you to remember and, ultimately, easy for your audience to follow. (Figure 7 is an illustration of a final outline, based on the rough outline shown in Figure 1.)

The purpose of an outline is to select and order your many thoughts, ideas, examples, illustrations, statistics, and quotations. It is useless to make an outline from a speech that is already written:

the outline must always come first. However, the outline should not become rigid until you have completed your thinking about the speech. The outline should be a changing thing. As you place your ideas in some kind of order, you can see when a point or a quotation does not fit or when you need additional information. This is one reason why placing your information on note cards will help you prepare your speech. The order can be easily changed and new data can easily be included. There are several suggestions to keep in mind that will help make outlining easier.

a. Determine the Major Points. A major point is a general statement putting forth one clear and distinct idea that supports, explains, or proves your purpose. Major points should never overlap in an outline. (For instance, in the outline shown in Figure 7, if point I., B. were to read "Affects his body," it would overlap point I., A.) Major points should never be stated as questions; they should always be declarative in form. As far as possible, all major points in an outline should be of equal importance.

Many times the pattern that you have chosen will determine your major points. If your pattern is problem-solution, your outline will probably have two major points, the first stating the problem and the second putting forth the solution. If your pattern is past, present, future, you will have three major points.

You must always have at least two major points. Major points are nothing more than subdivisions of your purpose, and you cannot divide something into one part. A student who by error submits an outline with only one major point has usually mistaken the purpose of his speech as the first major point. Although an outline must have at least two major points, it is seldom necessary to include more than five major points. A speech with more than five major points is usually a poorly arranged speech with overlapping ideas. The fewer the major points, the easier it is for the audience to understand. Most speeches lend themselves to two or three major points.

b. Determine the Subpoints. A subpoint supports, explains, or proves the point to which it is subordinated. Again, each point must be distinct and must not overlap any other point. Each major point must have at least two subpoints, each subpoint (if it is subdivided at all) must have at least two lesser points, and so forth on down the line. An outline should never have a I without a II or an A without a B, etc.

General Purpose: To persuade
Specific Purpose: To persuade about smoking
Narrowing the Purpose: Smoking is detrimental.
Stating the Purpose: I will persuade my audience that they should stop smoking or never start because smoking is detrimental to the smoker and to others.

Introduction: Have you ever lighted a cigarette, taken a deep drag, pulled the smoke deep into your lungs, and then released the smoke slowly? How did it feel? Did it give you a pleasurable experience? Did you really enjoy it? Really? The next time you feel as if you would like to smoke, take a single cigarette and look at it carefully and ask yourself, ''Is it worth fourteen minutes of my life?'' Yes, latest reports estimate that the average man reduces his life by fourteen minutes every time he smokes a cigarette. If you smoke two packs a day or more, you will live 8.3 years less. Today I would like to show you that smoking is detrimental both to you and to others.

I. Detrimental to the smoker
    A. Affects his health
        1. Causes cancer
            a. Lung cancer
                (1) 75% of lung cancers caused by smoking (Surgeon General's Report)
                (2) 52,000 die yearly (Surg. Gen. Rpt.)
                (3) Describe smoker's lung
                (4) Dr. Johnson's patients (Interview)
            b. Upper respiratory tract cancer
                (1) Lip, tongue, mouth, pharynx, larynx, esophagus (Am. Cancer Soc.)
                (2) Study of 185,000 men-seven times nonsmokers (Dept. H. E. W.)
            c. Urinary bladder cancer (Dept. H. E. W.)
        2. Causes chronic bronchopulmonary diseases
            a. Chronic bronchitis (Dept. H. E. W.)
            b. Pulmonary emphysema (Dept. H. E. W.)
        3. Causes cardiovascular diseases
            a. Mortality rate twice nonsmokers (Surg. Gen. Rpt.)
            b. Nicotine causes vasospasm or constriction of arteries (Am. Pub. Health Assoc.)

B. Affects his pocketbook
   1. Eight billion spent yearly (Am. Pub. Health Assoc.)
   2. One pack a day–$100+ a year
   3. Number of days lost from work (H. E. W.)
      a. One pack–48% more days than nonsmoker
      b. Two packs–83% more days than nonsmoker
   4. Increased medical costs
      a. Spends one third more time in hospital (Surg. Gen. Rpt.)
      b. Sees doctor twice as often (H. E. W.)

II. Detrimental to others
   A. Smoking causes accidents
      1. Smoking increases traffic accidents
         a. Smokers have more accidents (Am. Ins. Assoc.)
         b. Night vision affected
            (1) Tobacco amblyopia (H. E. W.)
            (2) Optic atrophy (Sur. Gen. Rpt.)
      2. Smoking causes fires
         a. 163,900 fires linked to smoking (H. E. W.)
            (1) $80,400,000 property loss
            (2) 1,800 deaths
         b. Burns to rugs, furniture, clothing (personal examples)
   B. Smoking harmful to unborn children
      1. Affects birth weight (H. E. W.)
      2. Linked to premature births, abortions, and/or stillbirths (Surg. Gen. Rpt.)
      3. Dr. Johnson's orders to mothers-to-be (Interview)

Conclusion: So the next time you pick up a cigarette, ask yourself if it is worth it. Is it worth dying from cancer, chronic bronchopulmonary diseases, or cardiovascular diseases? Is it worth the money it costs, the days lost from work, the money spent for hospital and doctor bills? If you don't care about yourself, is smoking worth an automobile accident or a fire in which you might kill someone you love? If you are a mother-to-be, is smoking worth what it might do to that unborn child? Yes, the next time you pick up a cigarette, throw it away, and breathe a little easier.

Figure 7. Final Outline.

c. Symbols and Spacing. A consistent set of symbols should always be used in outlining and these should always be properly spaced. The most common symbols are used as follows:

I. Roman numerals
  A. Capital letters
    1. Arabic numerals
      a. Lower-case letters
        (1) Arabic numerals in parenthesis
          (a) Lower-case letters in parenthesis

Beyond this point the symbol form varies. Usually the next step is to use brackets.

Notice that each subpoint is placed directly under the first letter of the first word of the point to which it is subordinated. In other words, point 1 (Arabic numeral one) is placed under the "C" in the word "Capital" of point A, the point to which it is subordinated. Each symbol should be followed by a period. Each symbol not enclosed in parentheses or brackets should be followed by two spaces. When symbols are enclosed, the two spaces follow the closing parenthesis or bracket. If a point in an outline is longer than one line, the second line begins under the first letter of the first word of the point.

Each symbol in a set of symbols should appear directly under the preceding symbol of the same series. In other words, all capital letters should be placed directly under each other, all Arabic numerals directly under each other, and so on. (See Figure 7.)

The outline should be single-spaced within major points and double-spaced between. For neatness, Roman numerals should be expanded to the left. All points in an outline should begin with a capital letter; they should end with a period if they are in sentence form. If the outline is written rather than typed, the spacing should be approximated.

d. Form. There are only three forms to use in outlining. An outline is either in single-word form, phrase form, or complete-sentence form. An outline using single words is discouraged, because a well-written outline should be meaningful to anyone for speaking; moreover, words are often ambiguous, and even the speaker can be puzzled when he sees them out of the context of his original thoughts. A phrase outline is easily read and lends itself readily for use as speaker's notes. A sentence outline features sentences which are as nearly parallel as possible within any one division of the outline. A sentence outline used for speeches to persuade may incorporate the word "because" or the word "for" after each point until the proof is reached. The entries in an outline should be consistent; the forms are not mixed.

C. The Conclusion

If you have summarized each major point of your outline, the important steps, information, or arguments have been properly placed before your audience at least once. The conclusion is your last opportunity to state the purpose of your speech and to identify the major issues. Like the introduction, the conclusion should be carefully planned. It should be short, to the point, written out, and possibly memorized. The conclusion should include a transition, a summary, and a concluding statement.

1. Transition. A statement is needed to introduce the conclusion and to inform your audience that they have another chance to listen to your major points. Direct phrases such as "In conclusion" or "In summary" alert the listener yet do not delay the progress of the conclusion itself. Avoid such statements as "I have tried" or "I have attempted today to . . ."; these are weak, apologetic statements, and the conclusion must be strong.

2. Summary. The main points of your speech belong in the conclusion. You may want also to repeat the essence of your major supporting arguments, so that any information that might have been missed or misunderstood in the body of the speech can be regained in the conclusion. Try to change in some way the expression of the points you repeat, for direct repetition of what you have said previously has a tendency to cause the audience to "tune out." Another good way to restate your important points is to reverse the order within each point. If you have presented as your first major point the idea that juvenile delinquency is a problem in America today, restate your main arguments in *support* of this point and then restate the major point. For example, you would point out that more juveniles are being arrested than ever before, more juveniles are addicted to drugs than ever before, and more unwed mothers are juveniles than ever before, and then conclude that for these reasons America must recognize the problem of juvenile delinquency. If you are demonstrating how to shine shoes, you may have started by shining the edge of the soles of the shoes. Repeat your *reasons* for starting with the soles and then reword the major point.

3. Concluding Statement. Many times, the audience does not know when a speaker has finished. For a short time there is an air of uneasiness in the room. Far too many speeches end with just a summary and no more. The summary should be followed with a final and concluding statement. The purpose of your speech should be placed before your audience once more. If you can incorporate a quotation or a few lines of poetry, all the better. If you have used a quotation in your introduction, either refer to it once more or continue with another part of it. Perhaps you used Shakespeare's "All the world's a stage, and all the men and women merely players" in your introduction. In the body of your speech you may have referred several times to the part every man must play in order to overcome a problem. In your conclusion you might refer once again to the quotation used in the introduction and continue with it: "Just as all men and women are merely players on the world's stage, 'They have their exits and their entrances,' it is now time for more of us to make an entrance. I hope you will agree with me that we should. . . ." Your final statement might very well be an appeal or a challenge to your audience. Whatever you use, be certain that it will assist in accomplishing your purpose and that it is easy to understand.

Your purpose should be stated generally in the introduction, specifically in the body, and then again generally, in different words, in the conclusion. The old saying is that you tell your audience what you are going to tell them in the introduction, you tell them in the body, and you tell them what you told them in the conclusion. The three divisions of a speech—introduction, body, and conclusion—complement one another.

SUMMARY

A speaker must find sources for the content of his speech, he must record the content, and he must organize the content. He may utilize three major sources of information: personal knowledge, the library, and personal interviews with authorities. This information may be recorded on note cards, in a notebook or folder, or by using the clipping method.

Once information is located and recorded, it must be properly organized according to three divisions: introduction, body, and conclusion. Each part of the speech must accomplish certain aims. The introduction must get the audience's attention, present the purpose, and include a transition into the body of the speech. The body of the speech should be developed point by point according to one of the seven patterns. The major points and subpoints should be arranged according to the form of a word, phrase, or sentence outline. The conclusion should present a transition, summarize the main ideas, and restate the purpose as well as round out the thought and conclude.

In preparing to speak, you first select an interesting subject; then you gather ideas and information and organize that information into a useful outline. Before you are ready to present your speech, you must word your ideas in such a way that they will be interesting and clear.

ASSIGNMENTS

1. Using the *Readers' Guide*, complete two source cards for each of the first five issues that you listed for assignment 5 in Chapter 1.
2. Locate editions of *Current History* and *Congressional Digest* that concern the first five issues you have listed. Complete a source card for each.
3. Locate at least one item in *Vital Speeches* that concerns the first five of your listed important issues. Complete a source card for each.
4. Looking ahead to your final speech, select three to five *general* areas about which you would like to learn more. These might be campus issues, local issues, state issues, or such national issues as pollution, taxes, welfare, politics, the draft, or any issue about which you are personally concerned. With the advice of your instructor select one general area about which you can start to gather information. No two students should select the same general areas. You may find that the assignments at the end of Chapter 1 will provide you with ideas.
5. When you have selected a general area, prepare a manila folder or envelope for your final speech topic. As you read magazines and newspapers, note articles that pertain to your final speech topic. Have copies made from library or loan materials. Place these articles in the folder or envelope.
6. Take a stand on one side of your final speech topic. State your stand in the form of a declarative statement. Check this statement with your instructor. When your topic has been approved by your instructor, prepare a "rough" outline. Check your outline with your instructor to make certain that all of the major points actually support your contention.

7. Prepare at least five source cards for your final speech topic. In addition, complete five quotation cards from each of the five source cards. Review the information concerning note taking. Check your cards with your instructor.
8. Prepare an attention-getting introduction for your final speech. Try various methods, including a word picture, startling statistics, and rhetorical questions. Check your introduction with your instructor.

chapter three
ORAL STYLE

There are only four ways to present a speech: by delivering it from memory, by reading it, by ad-libbing it, or by using the extemporaneous method. A few speeches are presented from memory, some speeches are read, but very seldom is a speech ad-libbed (given spontaneously without preparation). It is hoped that most of your speeches will be given extemporaneously. Using the extemporaneous method, you will complete the first steps described in Chapters 1 and 2: choose a subject, gather information, and make an outline. Unless the assignment calls for a sentence outline, you might wisely use a phrase outline, for this outline may function as the notes from which you speak. Because a phrase outline encourages you to record your ideas in a general way, you can rephrase your ideas as you practice your speech. A truly extemporaneous speech should be an ever changing thing. Using your phrase outline as a basis for what you want to say, rephrase your ideas, your examples, your illustrations each time you practice your speech. As you rephrase your ideas in an attempt to find the best possible way to express them, you are creating a style of your own. When you present your speech, the best possible way of saying what you want to say should come to mind. Thus the speech will have a sense of spontaneity.

Style brings together word choice, techniques, devices, and principles which make the difference between a forceful, effective speech and a dull, uninteresting one. Although the style you create will be determined by your own background, the subject of your speech, and the nature of the audience to whom you speak, there are some guides to help you create an effective style. Elements of style you can most profitably consider are word choice; principles of unity, coherence, and emphasis; and techniques of clarity, variety, and conciseness.

I. WORD CHOICE

Language is man's chief means of communication; it provides his means of thinking. As your power of word choice increases, your understanding increases. Your vocabulary increases as your daily experiences increase through participation and observation. As you see events taking place on television, hear about them on radio, or read about them in papers or magazines, learn new words and expressions. Try to read as many good books as possible; read from plays, histories, philosophies, and biographies. Make use of opportunities to talk with professional people, with people who have traveled extensively, with your instructors in conversation outside of class, and with your classmates who seem to excel. As you use these experiences to increase your vocabulary, your power of word choice increases. Three areas of word choice are especially important to examine: concrete words, slang words, and figurative words.

A. Choose Concrete Words

A speaker should attempt to use words that are concrete rather than abstract. The terms "abstract" and "concrete" are relative; for example, the range might move from abstract to concrete in the following way: a thing, a musical instrument, a viol, a violin, a Stradivarius. The wisest choice is the most concrete word possible. Because concrete things, places, plants, animals, people, exact quotations, specific figures, and personal experiences are far more interesting than vague generalities and abstract words, you should choose words that give listeners vivid, colorful, striking, and intense impressions. Such careful detail will make your speech more effective. For example, instead of saying "They say we don't have a population problem but I want you to know it's a terrible problem and could mean the end of us all," you might say, "According to the *Statistical Abstract*, if our population continues to grow at its present rate, by the year 2200 there will be one square foot of land for every individual." Samuel Clemens pointed out, "The difference between the right word and the almost right word is the difference between lightning and the lightning bug."

B. Evaluate Slang Carefully

Slang consists of striking, bizarre, and currently popular words and statements that are meant to shock. The best of slang is ingenious, particularly in speeches dealing with social criticism. Slang may produce a poignant clarity; however, you should consider that some slang words are an affront to the dignity and decorum of some audiences. For example, the very slang that might "turn on" a college audience might "turn off" their parents.

C. Use Effective Figurative Words

Figurative words can add vividness, interesting force, and emphasis to your speech. Figurative language may be a better way to show the relationships of ideas and thought than direct representation can. When figurative language is used wisely, it can greatly enrich the meaning of a statement. However, many figurative words are worn out and ineffective. A "dead" figure of speech fails to sharpen perception; in fact, it hinders communication. Such overused expressions are said to be trite. Trite expressions are easy to think of; in fact, if you use common, familiar, ready-made expressions, you do not have to face the problem of choosing words, but your meaning will be vague to your audience. Such expressions as "face the music," "hard as rock," "green with envy," and "quick as a flash" have become hackneyed and worn out; they no longer evoke interest. Do not be afraid to use fresh, stimulating figurative words but avoid those which you fear might be considered trite. The three most common figurative uses of words are metaphor, simile, and personification.

1. *Metaphor.* A metaphor is an implied comparison which imaginatively identifies one object with another completely dissimilar object and gives to the first object one or more qualities of the second. For example, the term "population explosion" compares the rapid population growth with the destructive force of a bomb.

2. *Simile.* A simile is a comparison introduced by "like" or "as." It compares two things that are different in most ways but which are strikingly alike in one way. For example, the expression "his mind is as filthy as a polluted stream" implies that both are unclean but are different in every other way.

3. *Personification.* A personification is a special kind of metaphor which points out a similarity between animate things and inanimate things. For example, the expression "the house spoke to us of better days" implies that the inanimate house has the animate ability to speak.

II. UNITY, COHERENCE, AND EMPHASIS

The outline from which you will work will be the basis for unity, coherence, and emphasis in your speech. As you work to phrase your ideas, you should attempt to bring a continuity to what you say.

A. Unity

In speaking as in writing, each sentence should express a single thought. Furthermore, each paragraph should relate to one topic, and the speech as a whole should consist of a discussion of one subject. This principle is important to remember. Speakers often introduce stories and other material that are not related to the subject of their speech.

B. Coherence

Speeches have acceptable coherence when their parts fit together easily and appropriately. Each sentence should be properly related to the sentence that precedes it and to the one that follows. Each paragraph and topic should likewise be related to the preceding one and to the following one. Transitional devices must be given careful consideration, so that the various parts of the speech are appropriately connected. The desired result is smooth, flowing thought.

C. Emphasis

The thoughts expressed in a speech should be developed and placed in such a way that the more important ones are given prominence. For example, an effort should be made to place the most important part of a sentence at the beginning or at the end, because first impressions and last impressions are remembered longest. Frequently, the close of a sentence provides the best opportunity for emphasis. One may emphasize his most important thoughts by repeating them or by developing them more fully than he does the less important parts of his speech. He may even tell his audience that a certain part of his speech is especially significant. An experienced speaker usually places his most important ideas near the end of his speech and emphasizes them with forceful words, with superior sentence construction, and with vivid examples.

III. CLARITY, VARIETY, AND CONCISENESS

Clarity, variety, and conciseness are essential for effective speech.

A. Clarity

The language used in a speech should possess instant intelligibility. The listeners have no dictionary at hand in which to look up unfamiliar words. They have no time to reflect upon the meaning of unduly long or complicated sentences; their thoughts must keep changing as the speaker goes on to express additional thoughts and feelings. If you must use unfamiliar words, you should offer familiar synonyms or explain the meaning of an unfamiliar term. Sentences should be so constructed that they make the speaker's meaning easy to grasp. In fact, sentences should be so constructed that the speaker's meaning *cannot* be misunderstood.

Clarity should be considered throughout the planning of a speech. Too many phases of a subject, too many incidents, too many characters introduced into a story, too many details can be confusing at times and often detract from the purpose of the speech. In general, directness and simplicity contribute to clarity. However, the simplicity must be masterly and not superficial.

B. Variety

Since uniformity eventually deadens, variety is important for an effective oral style. Variety can be added to a speech by the use of facts, statistics, quoted material, examples, short stories, selected descriptions, figures of speech, bits of humor, poetry, and in some situations the use of slang.

C. Conciseness

Conciseness of speech is important. The law of economy applies to the use of words just as it applies to the spending of money: a good speaker does not waste words. He does not talk at great length about trifles. In telling stories he does not include unnecessary incidents; in describing he does not include every detail; in persuading he does not overprove his contentions. Experiment with various expressions of the same idea and select the most direct, the most concise.

SUMMARY

The speaker perfects his speech by carefully choosing words; by applying principles of unity, coherence, and emphasis; and by using techniques to achieve clarity, variety, and conciseness. The period during which a speaker practices his speech should be one of experimentation. With adequate preparation and practice, he should be able to express his ideas with naturalness and spontaneity at the time he delivers his speech.

Once you have found effective expression for what you have to say, you are ready to develop your voice, your posture and movement, your speaker-audience relationship, and your poise.

ASSIGNMENTS

1. List ten metaphors or similes used in a single issue of *Current History* or *Congressional Digest.*
2. In an issue of *Vital Speeches* select a speech concerning a topic that you find interesting. Make a source card for the speech and in addition make a list of any unfamiliar words used by the speaker.

chapter four

VOCAL COMMUNICATION

One of the most important aspects of oral style is that it can be made more meaningful than written style. It is this fact that produced the great speeches of Demosthenes and Cicero, Patrick Henry and James Madison, John F. Kennedy and Martin Luther King, Jr. The writer works with written words and word arrangements only; but the speaker can add greatly to the power of the words he uses. He can speak them with effective volume, with appropriate rate, with meaningful pitch, and with stirring quality. In this chapter you will learn how to develop an effective speaking voice.

I. VOICE CONSCIOUSNESS

Many people give little thought to the manner in which they use their voices. They are not voice conscious. Consequently, they do not know whether their voices are acceptable or unacceptable. In fact, many people react with shock when they first listen to their voices on a tape recorder. Furthermore, most people do not know the characteristics of a superior speaking voice. A first step, then, in learning to use your voice well is to train yourself to sense the characteristics of voices that are inadequate or irritating and to distinguish the qualities that contribute to a pleasing, effective voice.

In training yourself to evaluate speaking voices, take an increased interest in the voices of the people around you. Are they pleasing or unpleasant? Note particularly the characteristics of the voices that are pleasing and expressive. If opportunity permits, study a number of recordings and note qualities that characterize the voices. Listen carefully and frequently to the best voices that you hear on radio and television. Seek to become a competent judge of voices. Your ear must become more sensitive to voice characteristics and you must become a competent judge of voices if you are to make effective progress in improving the use of your own voice.

II. VOICE PRODUCTION

Voice production consists of respiration, phonation, resonance, pronunciation, and articulation. All work together in a smoothly functioning process to produce speech.

A. Respiration

The speaking mechanism is a wind instrument, somewhat resembling a trumpet. This fact makes the use of breath an important part of voice production. Correct posture is an important part of breathing. The person who has poor posture is as handicapped upon occasions requiring good speech as is the individual who is too tense or nervous. In preparing to speak you should stand tall, maintain good posture, and use the entire body with alertness and spontaneity.

The breath travels from the lungs, which are made up of tiny air sacs, up the trachea, or windpipe, to the larynx. The air is expelled, or exhaled, from the lungs by the combined efforts of the diaphragm, abdominal muscles, and chest and rib muscles. When you inhale, the ribs are pulled up and out by the intercostal muscles and additional muscles attached to the thoracic wall. At the same time, the chest cavity is expanded in every direction, up and down, side to side, and front to back; the diaphragm, working with the abdominal muscles, flattens out. The raising of the ribs and the flattening of the diaphragm reduce the air pressure in the lungs. Simultaneously with the expansion, air rushes into the lungs, thereby equalizing the air pressure. When you exhale, the ribs move downward and inward, the diaphragm rises, the abdominal muscles relax, and the size of the thoracic cavity is reduced. This, in turn, increases the air pressure around the lungs and forces the air out of them.

Deep and well-regulated breathing is necessary for control of the volume, quality, rate, and, to some extent, the pitch of the voice. Acquiring the habit of deep and controlled breathing, in which the rhythm is adjusted to the rhythm of speech, is an important factor in learning to use your voice well.

B. Phonation

Phonation is the act of producing sounds. As the air travels up the trachea, no sound is made until it reaches the larynx. The larynx, located at the top of the trachea, consists of a series of cartilages containing the vocal folds, two ridges or folds of elastic tissue which project from the sides. These ridges or folds stretch across the larynx in a V-shaped formation to form a valve. In producing sound, the vocal folds tighten and draw together. The air from the lungs moves against the vocal folds, forcing them apart and causing their edges to vibrate. The vibration causes sound waves, which are molded into speech.

Effective voice production is possible only when the proper habit of relaxing the larynx has been established. (The larynx can best be relaxed by relaxing the muscles of the neck.) The effort needed for vigorous speech should be centered in the diaphragm and in the abdominal walls. You will get the best results by relaxing the larynx as much as the production of tone permits. You should not relax so completely, however, that the tone becomes weak, monotonous, or colorless. Try to use the degree of relaxation that best enables you to produce pleasing, effective tones. Habitual constriction of the throat must be overcome in order that the vocal mechanism can be a flexible instrument responding with appropriate tension for various types of expression.

C. Resonance

The sound leaving the vocal folds is relatively weak and lacks amplification. As chief resonators, the pharynx, the mouth, and the nasal passages assist in amplification. The resonators affect the voice somewhat as the body of a violin reinforces the faint sound made by a violin string, and as the tubes of various sizes and shapes affect the tones produced by certain wind instruments. Vocal sound consists of a combination of various types of air waves. The air waves modify and reinforce each other by means of resonation in such a way that a louder and more pleasing tone results. In improving your speech, you will wish to spend some time in forming better habits of adjusting and using your resonators in order that the richest, fullest, and most suitable tones possible may be produced. You will find, for instance, that the use of the resonators can often be increased when the vowels and the voiced consonants are deliberately sounded.

If the resonators are to do their best work, four factors must be considered in using them. These factors are relaxation, openness, forward placement, and nasal resonance.

1. Relaxation. You have already learned that undue tension must not be present if the larynx is to do its best work. This is equally true of the resonators. Unpleasant tones are often due to unneeded tension in one or more of the resonators. Tension is most often found in the pharynx (the throat). Relax the throat as much as possible. Suggestions for reducing bodily tension are found in Chapter 5.

2. Openness. Many people need to open their mouths wider when they speak. Optimum openness keeps the teeth and lips from muffling the tones. Opening the mouth sufficiently also results in a more open throat, thus improving resonance. Although opening the mouth to a certain point improves tone production, opening it beyond that point results in poorer tones. Openness should not be carried so far that it attracts attention to itself. It will be necessary for you to experiment in order to develop proper habits of openness.

3. Forward Placement. To produce tone, some people seem to center the effort in the area of the soft palate, the upper back of the mouth. This gives the effect of swallowing the tones. Others seem to center the effort in the throat. This may result in a hollow tone or in other types of displeasing voice quality. To overcome these defective uses of energy, you should concentrate on using the forward part of your mouth. You will obtain good results by being particularly conscious of the use of the hard palate, the soft palate, the uvula, the tongue, the teeth, the lips, and the jaws. The articulators will be discussed in more detail shortly.

4. Nasal Resonance. Many voices are unpleasant because too much or too little nasal resonance occurs. A voice characterized by too much nasality is said to be nasal. A voice lacking in nasality is denasal. There are three speech sounds that should be produced with an abundance of nasality: *m*, *n*, and *ng*. In the production of the other speech sounds little or no nasal resonance should occur.

Denasal tones are often produced when one has a cold. If they are produced at any other time, the nasal passages should be examined to find whether the nasal obstruction requires medical attention.

D. Pronunciation and Articulation

The final step in speaking is the molding of the sounds produced by phonation and resonation into the various sounds that compose language. The sounds are molded into language by the seven articulators: teeth, tongue, lips, jaws, hard palate, soft palate, and uvula. As you know, English sounds consist of vowels, consonants, and diphthongs. Vowels are speech sounds that are produced with relatively open articulators. Consonants are produced with articulators closed or relatively closed. A diphthong (for instance, *oi* as in *oil*, *ou* as in *out*, *i* as in *ice*) is two vowel sounds so spoken that there is continuous sound as one passes from the first vowel to the second; the first vowel is usually held longer and is given more stress than the second. The vocal folds vibrate during the production of all vowels but not during the production of all consonants.

Improper pronunciation and poor articulation interfere with communication. The way you speak should never divert attention from *what* you say.

It should be pointed out that pronunciation usually refers to the way a word is sounded in *isolation;* articulation concerns the way speech sounds are made during *continuous* speech.

1. Pronunciation. Correct pronunciation, the ability to produce the correct sounds in the right places with the proper stress, is based on usage. There are three principal varieties of American English spoken throughout the United States: Eastern, Southern, and General American. Eastern speech is heard in New England and among the educated of New York City. Southern speech is the speech of the Old South. General American speech is used west of the Hudson River and north and west of the Old South. *Each* of these varieties of American English is recognized as *standard* in the area in which it is spoken and is acceptable *anywhere.* Each dialect possesses merit and charm when it is spoken well. It is the *substandard* varieties of these dialects that should be avoided. Substandard varieties include speech that is carelessly pronounced. Unfortunately, the average American has substandard speech.

There are several errors in pronunciation to be considered: accent, substitution, insertion, omission, and transposition.

a. Accent. The relative stress given to the syllables of a word varies somewhat, but it is sufficiently permanent that unconventional use of stress forms one type of mispronunciation. There are only a few general rules concerning stress, and even they have many exceptions. For words read in books or magazines but rarely heard, the dictionary is the most reliable guide to pronunciation. For the pronunciation of commonly used words, educated speakers in your own area can be your guide. The following words are often mispronounced because of a misplaced accent: *ad* mirable, de *bate*, *im* potent, *in* famous, *mis* chievous, su *per* fluous, *the* ater, and *ve* hement.

b. Substitution. The substitution of one sound for another is a frequent error of pronunciation. Among the most common substitutions are the following:

d for *t* medal (for *metal*), pardner (for *partner*)

d for *th* dat (for *that*), dem (for *them*), dos (for *those*), wid (for *with*)

i for *a* agin (for *again*), kin (for *can*)

i for *e* git (for *get*)

i for *u* jis' and jist (for *just*)

th for *s* (commonly known as a lisp) betht (for *best*)

u for *aw* becuz and 'cuz (for *because*)

u for *o* fur (for *for*)

uh for *ow* yelluh (for *yellow*)

c. Insertion. A common error of pronunciation is the insertion of an additional sound or syllable.

inserted *a* athalete (for *athlete*), athaletics (for *athletics*)

inserted *e* Aperil (for *April*), umberella (for *umbrella*)

inserted *u* elum (for *elm*), filum (for *film*), tickulish (for *ticklish*)

inserted *y* fayast (for *fast*), layast (for *last*)

Words such as *often*, *toward*, and *subtle* frequently involve an insertion of sound for a silent letter.

d. Omission. Another error of pronunciation is the omission of sounds. Sounds are frequently omitted from the beginning, end, and middle of words.

Initial and Final Sounds

a omitted 'cross (for *across*), 'mong (for *among*)

d omitted worl' (for *world*), ban' (for *band*)

g omitted goin' (for *going*), bein' (for *being*)

t omitted slep' (for *slept*), kep' (for *kept*)

th omitted 'at (for *that*), 'em (for *them*)

Medial Sounds (These words are frequently mispronounced. They should be recognized and memorized so that the errors are avoided.)

adjetive (for *adjective*)
goverment (for *government*)
hunerd (for *hundred*)
libary (for *library*)
picher (for *picture*)
probly (for *probably*)
literture (for *literature*)
sophmore (for *sophomore*)

e. Transposition. In a few cases, the sounds within a word are transposed.

calvary (for *cavalry*)
irrevelant (for *irrelevant*)
larnyx (for *larynx*)
preformed (for *performed*)

2. *Articulation.* Articulation (or enunciation, as it is sometimes called) is concerned with the distinctness or clarity of continuous speech. Improper articulation is the inaccurate formation of vowels and consonants in fluent speech. A speaker is guilty of poor articulation when he knows how to pronounce the words correctly but fails to do so because of habit, carelessness, laziness, or indifference. A speaker is said to articulate correctly when his sounds and words are clearly made and easily understood, without their being overly precise. Major articulation errors are concerned with poor quality and excessive assimilation.

a. Quality. If your voice lacks resonance, is low in volume, or is excessively nasal, throaty, or guttural, it can be very difficult to understand what you say. In some cases, these faults can be corrected only by surgery. However, proper breathing, proper training, and proper exercises can usually help overcome such faults. Your first step might be to visit a speech clinic.

b. Excessive Assimilation. Assimilation occurs when sounds are influenced by other sounds. A certain amount of assimilation occurs in all speech. Americans have a tendency to speak rapidly and to say words as easily as possible. When we economize to an extreme, when speech becomes mumbled or slovenly, it is usually due to excessive assimilation. Some of the errors of excessive assimilation are similar to those found in mispronunciations. The difference is that mispronunciations occur in isolation; excessive assimilations occur during continuous speech. Most examples of excessive assimilation occur as substitutions, omissions, or a combination of substitutions and omissions.

Substitutions

aw for *al* awready, awright
it for *at* lookit
of for *have* couldof, wouldof, shouldof
ta for *to* oughta

Omissions

(initial sounds) er (for *her*), im (for *him*), em or um (for *them*), cuz (for *because*), cho or cha (for *you*), ud (for *would*)

(medial sounds) wunt (for *wouldn't*), shunt (for *shouldn't*), kunt (for *couldn't*)

(final sounds) goin (for *going*), comin (for *coming*), doin (for *doing*), yur or yuh (for *you*), don (for *don't*)

Combinations

gonna (for *going to*)	howdja (for *how did you*)
hafta (for *have to*)	wyncha (for *why don't you*)

There are many more examples of excessive assimilation found in rapid and careless speech. Look for examples in the speech of your classmates and in your own speech. Make a list of the articulation errors you discover. Remember, however, that many examples of assimilation are not only acceptable but necessary and preferred. The word *the* often properly becomes *thuh*; and *a*, which is usually pronounced as a long *a*, often becomes *uh* in continuous speech.

Overarticulation results in "stilted" speech. If you decide that your articulation is excessively assimilated and results in mumbled or slovenly speech, determine whether the errors are substitutions, omissions, or combinations. Articulate carefully; listen to yourself speak; and if possible use a tape recorder to help you mark your progress.

III. VOCAL VARIETY

Your voice can become a much more effective instrument of communication if you vary your rate of speaking, employ a wider pitch range, and use changes in volume. When you speak, variations in the rate, pitch, and volume carry meaning just as your words do. You will find it helpful to notice how vocal variety conveys meaning when used by speakers who appear on television and radio and in movies.

A. Rate of Speaking

The rate of speaking refers to the overall tempo or pace of speaking. Three phases of rate need to be considered: grouping, pausing, and duration.

1. Grouping. You are familiar with the hesitant and broken speech that occurs when a child is learning to read. You may have heard the halting speech of one who is learning a new language. Grouping should be such that it aids in conveying meaning accurately and clearly. When we have acquired a satisfactory command of our language, we are inclined to group words that express a single idea, just as we group syllables into a single word. Grouping may consist of a few words or of several words.

In speech and in oral reading, grouping may be unsatisfactory when the speaker is uncertain of himself, confused, or tired. One should keep in mind that not *all* trained speakers group their words in the same way and that the same speaker may vary his grouping of the same words on different occasions or when repeating a statement. A speaker's grouping of words should be considered satisfactory if it conveys the meaning *he* intends to convey.

2. Pausing. Pauses between word groups help to make a speaker's meaning clear; for that reason they are often referred to as vocal punctuation. The pause also may be used to give emphasis or to allow the audience time to grasp the speaker's meaning and to respond to what he has just said.

The effective speaker is not hesitant when he pauses. He is mentally alert and emotionally responsive. Although the speaker often uses the pauses to take inconspicuous sips of air, no extraneous sounds should occur during the pauses. Ineffective speakers often form the habit of saying "uh," "ah," "anduh," or similar meaningless "vocal pauses" when they speak. This is a common error which is very distracting. Learn to use pauses effectively; they should be a deliberate effort to create clarity or emphasis.

3. Duration. Meaning can be expressed by the length of time a speaker takes to say the vowels and many of the consonants. Note how saying the following words quickly helps to express the meaning of the words: *hurry, little, quick, run, short.* Now note how the meaning of the following words can be expressed by saying them slowly: *float, heavy, long, slow.*

If we speak too rapidly, it is hard for our listeners to grasp what we say. On the other hand, if we speak too slowly, listeners are annoyed at the slow pace.

The person who clips his speech needs to extend the duration of his sounds to the point at which they become acceptable; one who drawls needs to say words more quickly.

B. Pitch

Pitch is the relation of sound to the musical scale. Among the factors that determine the pitch of an individual's speech are the rapidity with which the vocal folds vibrate, the length of the vocal folds, and the thickness of the vocal folds. An analysis of pitch includes a discussion of range, key, inflection, and step.

1. Range. The use of a relatively wide pitch range makes speech more meaningful and interesting. Excitement and joy are among the emotions generally expressed in relatively high pitch. On the other hand, sadness and contentment are generally expressed in relatively low pitch. A speaker who uses little or no range variation in his pitch soon loses the attention of his audience.

2. Key. The predominant pitch that occurs during speech is called the key. One's voice mechanism functions best in a key that is about one third of the way from the bottom of his natural pitch range. Most of us speak in a key that is above the optimum. With a little effort and practice, anyone's key can be lowered slightly.

3. Inflection. The pitch glides that are placed on speech sounds, words, and phrases are called inflection. Upward inflections tend to occur in questioning, in pausing before a complete thought has been expressed, and during excitement. Downward inflections usually occur at the end of declarative sentences, when commands are given, and when certainty is expressed. Circumflex inflections, which occur when the pitch moves upward and downward, or downward and upward, are often heard when ridicule is expressed, when statements are insincere, and when certainty and incomplete thought appear together. Many different ideas and moods are expressed by means of inflection.

4. Step. The step occurs when pitch is changed as a speaker passes from syllable to syllable or from word to word. The step is most often used when ideas and emotions change and when varying emphasis is used.

C. Volume

Many people fail to make effective use of volume. They speak so softly that they cannot be easily heard, so loudly that the sound is distracting or even painful, or they fail to vary the volume. Volume should be adjusted to the number of people present and to the distance they are seated from the speaker. Volume should vary to suit the ideas and feelings that are being expressed.

SUMMARY

To accomplish effective vocal communication, a speaker must always be voice conscious. Not only must he listen for vocal characteristics in the voices of others, but, more important, he must be aware of his own voice. He should know that acceptable voice production consists of proper respiration, phonation, resonance, pronunciation, and articulation.

The speaker must realize that deep, well-regulated breathing is necessary for acceptable speech. He must be aware that the larynx needs to be relaxed and flexible if he is to phonate properly. He must know that if speech lacks proper amplification, it is difficult to hear and understand. A good speaker must avoid such errors in pronunciation as improper accent, substitution, insertion, omission, and transposition. He should know that poor quality and excessive assimilation must be avoided for proper articulation. Above all, vocal variety is necessary for proper vocal communication. If a speaker fails to vary the rate, pitch, and volume of his speech, he will soon find that he cannot communicate effectively with his audience.

If a speaker properly regulates his breathing, relaxes his throat, amplifies his sound, pronounces and articulates carefully, and has vocal variety, he will accomplish effective vocal communication.

ASSIGNMENTS

1. From TV or radio "talk" shows, select a speaker who you feel has an outstanding voice. List the vocal characteristics that made you select this speaker.
2. Make a list of ten mispronounced words that you hear during any single day.
3. Prepare a short (thirty seconds to one minute) report on any topic. Your instructor will record the reports on a tape recorder. Be certain to include your name as part of the report.
4. Listen to the reports recorded for assignment 3. Before playing each report, your instructor will assign someone other than the person who recorded the report to take notes on the report. After each report, the person taking notes will discuss any pronunciation or articulation errors in the report.

chapter five

VISUAL COMMUNICATION

You have probably noticed that a speaker's general appearance, posture, gestures, movements, and facial expressions convey ideas and express emotions that either help clarify what he is saying or detract from the effect of his words. Students of speech soon become aware of the importance of good visual communication between themselves and their audience. They become interested in how they look; in appearing self-confident and friendly; in movements, gestures, and facial expressions that suggest ease, naturalness, and alertness; in the proper way to look at an audience when delivering a speech; and in acquiring poise. In short, a speaker is not only heard; he is also seen. His audience will grasp the meanings that he expresses by means of both auditory and visual impressions.

I. GENERAL APPEARANCE

The way in which a speaker appears to his audience may determine the relationship he can establish with them. Although the trend on most college campuses is toward informality, there remain some occasions for which a speaker must plan his appearance to please a sophisticated audience. Evaluate the appearance of speakers on your campus. Speakers who have a sincere reason for speaking are seldom willing to jeopardize their effectiveness by appearing in a condition which might alienate their audience. Thus it is that once again you should consider the subject, the occasion, and the audience. Your objectives should be to please your audience, to appear natural, and to be comfortable.

II. POSTURE

Good posture has always been recognized as an aid in speaking. In the most general sense, good posture not only creates an *impression* of confidence but is also a first step to *self*-confidence. People tend to assume that a speaker who cannot face his audience straight and tall is apologetic, insecure, or unprepared. Specifically, a speaker must maintain good posture in order to breathe properly; breath control is, of course, essential for effective speech. Good posture also creates an optimum line for eye contact with the audience, and it aids in the comfortable use of gestures.

Allied to good posture are a number of suggestions that may help you to be more comfortable in a speaking situation.

Pace your walk to the rostrum. Walking too rapidly speaks of undue haste, of thoughtless impulse, and possibly of fear. On the other hand, walking too slowly may suggest dread of meeting the speaking situation or lack of readiness to speak.

When you reach the rostrum, pause just a few seconds to relax, to establish a normal breathing pattern, and to give your audience time to get a good view of you; the audience looks before it listens.

Try to relax. Your back should be straight, but not stiff. Your hands should hang relaxed at your sides when you are not gesturing or handling visual aids. Ideally, your weight should be balanced on both feet. Do not shift your weight from foot to foot while you speak, for this is a very distracting movement.

III. MOVEMENT

Many speakers walk about very little as they speak; others walk about rather freely. The point to remember is that there should always be *purpose* behind whatever movement a speaker uses. A speaker may take a few steps toward his audience, may walk about as he relates to the various sections of his audience, or may take a few steps as he demonstrates a visual aid. However, aimless pacing is a distraction.

A speaker's freedom to move may depend on the circumstances and the speech. For example, the need to use a stationary microphone or the presence of a television camera may curtail movement. If free to move, a speaker may lean forward a bit as he talks earnestly to his audience, or he may lean back as he relaxes at the end of a thought. A speaker may wish to step backward as he finishes the discussion of a major point, or to step forward or to the side as he begins the discussion of a new point. Movement forward is usually for emphasis. Movement to the side, and at times forward, is usually for transition.

There should be little movement during the early part of a speech. Movement on the part of a speaker should gradually cease as he nears the end of his speech. As his words and his voice suggest that he is about to finish, so should his movements.

IV. GESTURES

Gestures are *purposeful* movements designed to aid in expressing ideas or feelings. A speaker should be familiar with the types of gestures and with the principles relating to the use of gestures.

A. Types of Gestures

There are three types of gestures: emphatic, descriptive, and symbolic. Gestures should be varied throughout the speech. Never use the same hand for all gestures and do not repeat one gesture excessively. On the other hand, do not stand with your hands at your sides throughout the speech. Use appropriate gestures in *moderation.*

1. Emphatic Gestures. Experienced speakers often reinforce their words with emphatic gestures. Such gestures as clenching the fist, pointing the finger, and waving the hand are used to make it clear that what the speaker is saying is particularly important.

2. Descriptive Gestures. The hands and arms are often used to express size, shape, movement, number, and location. Descriptive gestures are especially useful for informative speeches. However, they may be used in any type of speech.

3. Symbolic Gestures. There are certain gestures to which meaning has been ascribed and which are understood by all. Shrugging the shoulders, shaking the head in negation, and nodding the head in approval are just a few of the symbolic gestures that are internationally intelligible.

B. Principles Concerning Gestures

Gestures should be natural and should be felt from within; they should be neither memorized nor mechanical. When you practice your speech and you feel that you would like to gesture, try various gestures until you find one that feels natural. Then, when you are speaking before your audience, forget about the gestures. If you know your speech well enough, gestures will come of their own accord. Underlying the use of gestures are some principles which may help you.

1. Appropriateness to the Words Being Used. Use gestures that express the same meaning as the words being used. This is essentially a mark of unity. For example, a clenched fist belongs with words of anger or challenge; shrugging the shoulders might accompany words of indecision. Gestures should at all times be appropriate.

2. *Timing.* Gestures should either slightly precede or accompany the words they are to reinforce. Poor speakers sometimes follow words with gestures. Comedians purposefully follow words with gestures because such inappropriate use of gestures is a source of amusement to the audience.

3. *Appropriateness to the Occasion.* You should consider, as you prepare to speak, whether the occasion calls for frequent and expressive gestures or for appropriate restraint. Vigorous gestures are helpful at athletic rallies; few gestures should occur during a memorial service. Similarly, before a small audience a speaker generally uses fewer gestures than he would use in speaking to a large crowd.

4. *Purposefulness.* All gestures should have a purpose. Small, jerky, "fuzzy" movements of the hands and arms are distractions. Such movements are called "half gestures" and should be avoided. Most gestures should be made in an area above the waist and below the head. Do not look at your own gestures, for you thereby give the audience the impression that you are more interested in your gestures than in what you are saying, or that you have forgotten what you intended to say next. A definite gesture is a complete gesture and should include the entire body. This does not mean that the gesture should be so vigorous that the entire body moves, but that the entire body should lend itself to what the gesture is trying to say. For example, the entire body may assume a powerful, determined attitude to accompany a clenched fist; the upper body may lean back from an extended arm and open palm meant to show expansive area. The body should support gestures.

5. *Gracefulness.* Movements that are awkward, jerky, or unduly angular should be adjusted to avoid unfavorable attention. If the entire arm is used for a gesture, the action should start with the elbow. The final result should be that your elbows are not held too close to your body nor are your arms extended too far as you gesture.

6. *Moderation.* The law of economy applies to gesturing as it does to all other phases of speaking. Try not to remind your audience of a statue, nor of a windmill.

V. FACIAL EXPRESSIONS

Your face is the most expressive part of your body. Fortunately, if you are concentrating on your message, the chances are that your facial expressions will be adequate. If you are poorly prepared or extremely frightened, your face will be the first place to show your inadequacy. Your face usually reflects your inner thoughts and not only helps you to express what you are trying to say but helps you to establish rapport with your audience. However, some speakers will not let their faces express what they really feel; they seem to work hard to keep their faces immobile as they deliver an entire speech "deadpan." If you are delivering a happy thought—smile. If something is serious, do not be afraid to let your face reflect that seriousness. Again, these expressions should not be planned but should be natural; they should be sincerely felt.

VI. WHERE TO LOOK

Just as your face is the most expressive part of your body, your eyes are the most expressive part of your face. The audience should see your eyes as much as possible. Look *into* the *eyes* of your audience, not over the audience, under the audience, through the audience, or to one side of the audience. Do not look at their foreheads, their noses, or their chins—meet their eyes.

Many speakers speak in such a way that listeners feel as if they are overhearing a private conversation rather than being directly addressed by the speaker. This does not mean that your voice should not be conversational in tone; it means that you should speak *to* your audience and not to the floor, the ceiling, the window, or the door.

Everyone in the audience should have the feeling that you are speaking directly to *him.* However, do not systematically look at every individual in the audience; simply give the impression that you are looking at everyone. This can be accomplished by scanning the audience. You should usually deliver at least one complete thought or illustration to one part of your audience, then look for a time at a nearby section of listeners as you say a few additional sentences. Gesture and look toward one side, direct a comment to the middle, and then speak to the other side. However, do not look back and forth so that you appear as a windshield wiper to the audience. Use moderation.

If you are using a microphone, be certain to have it positioned high enough to pick up your words yet low enough so that it will not block your face. Modern microphones are so sensitive that they can be several inches from your face and still catch every word. The important thing to remember is to keep looking at your audience. Do not look down at the microphone and do not let the microphone keep you from scanning your audience.

If you are speaking before a television camera, look up and speak to the camera just as you would to the audience. You will be told exactly where to look, and the red light will tell you which camera is being used.

If you are using note cards, an outline, or visual aids, look up as much as possible and scan your audience as much as possible. Do not let the note cards distract. If you need the information on the card, bring the card up at an angle so that you can see it without its obstructing the audience's view of your face. If you are using an outline or a manuscript from which to speak, have your speech well enough in mind that you can look up at least as much as you look down. (Additional suggestions may be found in Chapter 8 as part of "Interpretation.")

Remember that the audience reacts to the speaker, and in turn the speaker reacts to the audience. Not only should your audience see you, but you should see your audience. Speak to your audience and let them "speak" to you.

VII. POISE

A person who looks calm and at ease in a speaking situation has self-control. He is poised; he has control of himself both mentally and physically.

A. Mental Control

Most speakers experience some fear when they appear before an audience; in fact, some fear is beneficial. Controlled fear causes the mind to be more alert than usual; it brings the speaker to a high emotional pitch. The speaker can control stage fright through confidence; he gains confidence by being well prepared and having the right mental attitude.

1. Preparation. It is hoped that most of your speaking will be extemporaneous—that is, that you will have thought through your ideas, prepared an excellent outline, and practiced your speech several times from the outline you have prepared. In most speaking situations, the speech should not be memorized. On the other hand, it might be a good idea to memorize your outline. If the outline has been well prepared, your ideas are clear, well organized, and follow logically from point to point. A good outline should make it possible for anyone to give the same basic speech.

Many beginning speakers find that they are most frightened when they begin to speak; therefore, you may find it beneficial to memorize your introduction. You will find that after twenty or thirty seconds your fear will decrease and your mind will take over again. You will be in control of yourself once again.

2. *Positive Attitude.* How many times have you been advised to think positively? Positive thinking is an extremely important prelude to a speaking situation. Your first two or three speeches usually are relatively simple speeches. It may not seem at the time you get the assignments that they are easy, but when you look back later you will see that they were actually rather simple. Your first speech will be about a subject you know well—yourself. Obviously you will have little or no trouble with your first speech. If you realize that both your confidence and your ability will increase with every speaking experience, you should have a positive attitude.

B. Physical Control

The person who seems to be poised looks poised. Knowing that everyone has stage fright to some degree, one of the best things you can do is avoid making obvious the fact that you are frightened. If your hands shake, by all means neither hold papers in your hands nor hold your hands in such a way that the audience can see them shake. If your knees shake, you may want to walk about; however, try to synchronize your movements with a transition. Above all, it will help if you stand straight and tall and look at your audience. If you have good posture and good eye contact, and if you appear neat and pleasant, you will at least give the impression that you are poised. Deep breathing and exercises will help you to maintain physical control.

1. *Breathing.* One of the best things you can do before giving a speech is to breathe deeply and exhale *slowly* several times. This has a tendency to relax the entire body and especially the area of the throat. Never make taking a deep breath obvious if you are within view of the audience and especially if you are in front of a microphone. If your posture is good, no one should be able to tell when you use this exercise to relax.

2. *Exercises.* If you are in a position in which you cannot be seen by the audience, tense and relax your muscles. Put the palms of

your hands together and push against them and relax them several times. Tense your leg muscles and relax them. If you are familiar with isometric exercises, they are excellent to use before you speak.

VIII. VISUAL AIDS

Properly used, visual aids enhance a speech. They hold the audience's attention with a reinforcement of what is being said. Use of visual aids has a tendency to relax a beginning speaker. If he manipulates aids such as charts or graphs, he may feel comfortable in that he has something to do with his hands. Every speaker should be aware of the types of visual aids and some general rules for using them.

A. Types of Visual Aids

Anything that the speaker uses during his speech to illustrate in the physical sense can be called a visual aid. Aids may be divided into four types.

1. Actual Articles. If the article about which you are speaking can be brought to class, plan to use it as a visual aid, especially if you are giving a demonstration speech. If you are going to demonstrate how to grasp a tennis racket or how to swing it, both you and your audience profit by actually seeing the racket. If you are demonstrating a swimming stroke or the bandaging of a broken arm, ask a classmate to assist you.

2. Models. If it is impractical to bring the actual article to class, perhaps your subject can be shown in a scale model. Be sure the model is truly representative and large enough to be easily seen. A model of an atomic reactor or a doll in place of a baby will certainly assist in giving a speech to educate or demonstrate.

3. Maps, Charts, Drawings, Pictures. Some subjects make profitable the use of maps, charts, drawings, or pictures. Although the blackboard is excellent for fast, easy sketches, drawings completed on poster board are preferable if the topic is complex or involved. Pictures are excellent visual aids; if you have trouble finding the right picture, check with the library.

A persuasive speech especially lends itself to the use of visual aids, for nothing persuades like facts and figures, and nothing illustrates these better than graphs, charts, maps, and diagrams.

4. Projection Devices. Slide projectors, opaque projectors, filmstrips, and movies are often used by professional speakers and teachers. However, such devices do not lend themselves to short speeches given in speech classes. There are exceptions, of course; but in general, projection devices take proportionally too long to set up and to take down for the brief use they have in a classroom speech.

B. Rules for Using Visual Aids

Never use so many visual aids that they detract from the speech. Feel free to draw or make your own visual aids. They do not have to be works of art or perfect models to aid your speech. As you use visual aids, keep the following points in mind.

1. *Performability.* If your visual aid is to perform some activity, make certain that it is in working order. There is nothing more embarrassing than to show a working model that fails to work. Check it out just before your speech, if this is possible. If the aid uses batteries, make certain they are fresh.

2. *Size.* Make certain your visual aid is large enough to be seen easily by everyone in your audience. Avoid small pictures, especially pictures in a book. On the other hand, a visual aid that is larger than necessary will tend to look ridiculous. Use moderation.

3. *Appropriateness.* Above all, make certain the visual aids you use are appropriate. There is nothing so distracting as to watch a speaker use a visual aid and to wonder what the aid has to do with what he is saying. The aid should *aid.*

4. *Displaying.* If possible, keep your aid out of sight until you use it. An aid has a tendency to distract unless it is being used. One mistake of beginning speakers is to hold a book, or keep a finger in a book, for almost the entire speech. The audience will want to know what it is that the speaker has there. In addition, do not continue to display the aid after you have shown it. If you are going to refer to the same aid again, reintroduce it when the time comes. If it is necessary to use the aid frequently during the speech, the chances are that too much reliance is being placed on the aid. On the other hand, if the aid is rather large, do not make an attempt to remove it.

5. *Presentation.* When you are showing the aid, stand to one side or hold the aid to the side. Do not hold it in front of you so that you are forced to look down, for this destroys speaker-audience relationship and has a tendency to cause the speaker to mumble. If you hold the aid, try to keep one hand free for pointing to specific parts of the aid. If you are not holding the aid, stand to one side. Above all, do not turn your back to the audience to demonstrate something at the board. Do not stand in front of the aid if you are using it. Feel free to use a pointer.

6. Passing the Aid. Do not pass visual aids around the audience while you are speaking. If another speaker is to follow you, do not pass the aids around after you have finished. If a member of the audience is that interested in the aid, he will contact you at a later time.

SUMMARY

What the audience sees is just as important as what it hears. A good speaker should maintain acceptable posture at all times; he should use deliberate movements and gestures; his facial expressions should be meaningful; he should look directly at his audience; he should be poised; and he should use visual aids properly. These attributes of visual communication are closely related to oral communication. If the visual impression given to the audience is ineffective, the words spoken will be less than effective. Effective visual communication will enhance oral communication.

ASSIGNMENTS

1. Prepare a short talk (thirty seconds to one minute). Deliver the speech to the class and include as many gestures as possible.
2. Give a short speech (less than one minute). *Without* making any gestures, describe how to get from where you are presently living to the classroom.

chapter six

LISTENING

Communication takes place only when there is a speaker, a message, and a listener. A speaker should discover the best way to prepare and deliver his message, and he should let his audience "speak" to him by observing their facial expressions, their reactions, and their attitudes. Ideally an audience stimulates a speaker to think and talk more efficiently and effectively than he would without audience response. The listener plays a vital role in a speaking situation; it is with him that the ultimate effects of the speech are measured.

Hearing and listening are not necessarily the same. Hearing involves the process by which sound waves enter the ears. Listening is more than just hearing; it is the comprehension of what is said, and it should result in mental reaction. In other words, although people hear sounds during all of their waking hours, it is how these sounds affect their minds that is important. Hearing may be defined as auditory perception of sounds. Listening is actually the interpretation of the sounds that are heard.

Although people hear sounds continually, they comprehend and interpret those sounds for only a few minutes of any listening hour. Unless a listener deliberately concentrates on listening, he will neither comprehend nor interpret efficiently. The following suggestions are designed to help you to take more efficient notes and to be a more efficient listener.

I. PREPARATIONS

When you anticipate that a listening experience will occur, either as an assignment or because you have chosen to listen, advance preparations will make the experience more pleasant and more rewarding. Preparations for a listening experience include developing a proper attitude, doing some research about the speaker and/or his subject, and making provisions for taking notes.

A. Proper Attitude

If you look upon listening as a waste of time, if you feel that it isn't necessary to listen to the other speakers in class, if you find that you talk more than you listen, possibly a change in attitude is necessary. Actually we spend more of our time in listening than in talking, reading, and writing all put together. Most of what we learn we learn from listening. To listen with the best results, you must want to listen. Psychic deafness may result when listeners are emotionally disturbed and do not wish to hear. Listening efficiency is dulled by indifference, fault-finding attitudes, dislike for the subject, dislike for the speaker, and antagonism. Try to approach every listening situation with an open mind and with the attitude that every listening experience is actually a learning experience.

B. Preliminary Research

If you have been asked to evaluate a speaker, either in class or as an out-of-class assignment, you can improve your ability to listen effectively by doing some preliminary research. In most cases you will know in advance the subject of the speech that you are to hear. Gather as much specific information about the topic as possible. If the speaker has announced the areas he will cover within his speech, attempt to get some information in the areas about which you know the least. Read articles and books on the subject. Ask questions of others. You might make a rough outline of what you know about the subject and then supplement the weaker parts of your outline.

Try to find out as much as possible about the speaker beforehand. Learning something about his background may help you to understand his views and opinions. If the speaker is well known, you might try to locate reviews of previous speeches. Ask others for their views concerning the speaker and his subject.

C. Preparations for Note Taking

Students have been known to go into a listening assignment without any provisions for taking notes. Do not assume that you can remember all that was said or how it was delivered. Take with you at least two pens and a supply of paper with a solid back, perhaps a legal pad or a notebook.

If you are listening to a speech as an assignment, be certain that you know exactly what is expected of you. If you are to report on both content and delivery, divide your notes accordingly. If possible, prepare a critique form before you attempt a listening assignment. Place headings or topics on the form to help you organize notes as you take them. If you have been asked to comment on the various aspects of delivery, you might very well divide your form according to the topics on which you are to report: posture, gestures, movement, speaker-audience relationship, poise, and vocal delivery. In addition, list subtopics as part of the topics. You are, in effect, preparing a guide that will help you to look for the various aspects *as they happen.* If you are to report on content, add the headings of introduction, body, and conclusion. More information concerning the note taking at the time of delivery will be given as another part of this chapter.

II. EFFICIENT LISTENING

Ideally, every speaking situation would feature a poised, efficient, experienced speaker delivering a well-organized speech in an interesting manner. This, however, is not always the case. Some of the time, listening to a speech can become not only tedious but hard work as well. However, by listening with an open mind, by listening analytically, and by taking careful notes, you can make listening a rewarding experience.

A. Listen with an Open Mind

Not only should you try to have an open mind concerning the speaker and his topic before you attempt to listen, but you must also keep an open mind while you listen. Generally speaking, personal feelings, ideas, and opinions should not influence the notes you take. Many speeches that you hear will be of a controversial nature, will have two or more sides to the issue being discussed. It is very difficult to be unbiased before you listen to a speech; it is even more difficult to be unbiased when you hear a speaker disparaging or refuting your most cherished ideas and opinions. The important thing in listening is to get all that you possibly can from what the speaker is saying, while he is saying it. Do not try to argue with him or refute his opinions in your own mind while he is talking. When this happens, you become so emotionally involved that you may forget to listen carefully and to take careful notes. Try to realize that everyone is entitled to his opinion and that there is no institution that is beyond constructive criticism.

B. Listen Analytically

As you listen to a speaker, listen to both what he says and how he says it.

1. Analyze What Is Said. Make every attempt to follow the major points of the speech. A speaker usually gives some idea of the organization in his introduction by saying such things as "There are three things to be discussed," "There are two roads down which we may travel," or "There are five steps to be considered." As soon as possible analyze the overall organizational pattern of the speech.

Analyze how the speaker supports his major points. Does he list his subpoints? Does he support his points with evidence? Does he use facts, opinions, examples, figures of speech? If he uses facts, does he document his facts? Does he cite sources, give dates, use more than one source? If he uses opinions, are they his own opinions or those of someone else? If he uses his own opinions, does he supplement them with the opinions of others? Does he establish the fact that the person cited is an authority, an unbiased authority? Does he mention where the information can be found in print, when it was published or delivered, under what circumstances, at what time?

Does the speaker make emotional appeals? Does he vividly describe scenes, cite happenings, or tell stories that make you sad or happy? Does the speaker use general terms? Does he use expressions such as "they say" or "everyone knows"? Do the emotional appeals add to the speech? Do they help you understand what is being said, or do they simply appeal to your emotions?

In addition to analyzing the source and the quality of the speaker's evidence and the extent to which the speaker uses emotional appeals, you can note whether the speaker discusses the subject frankly, fairly, accurately, and with suitable proportion, or whether he misrepresents the facts; uses unsound reasoning; or exaggerates, minimizes, or avoids the discussion of important phases of the subject. You can think through a speaker's point to its many applications. You can study the various relationships of the statements made by the speaker. You can do all of these things and still comprehend all that the speaker is saying. In a sense you are making use of what the speaker says as he says it. As long as you are concerned with what a speaker says, your mind will not wander from the subject.

2. Evaluate Presentation. Listen to the way in which the speaker says what he says. Many times a person will say one thing but will try to indicate that he really means something else. Listen for the speaker's use of emphasis, of pauses, of changes in volume, pitch, and rate. Look for facial expressions. Does the speaker make a statement and shrug his shoulders, wrinkle his nose, or make some other movement or gesture which shows his true feelings concerning what he has just said? Does the speaker look at his audience when he speaks? Does he look sincere? Although this certainly does not mean that he is sincere, some speakers are unable to look at their audience when they are not sincere. The way something is said is just as important as what is said. This is one reason why a speech that was a thrilling experience when you heard it may seem dead and lifeless when you read it in the papers the next day.

C. Take Careful Notes

As has been mentioned, any prior preparation for note taking will certainly make the job easier. If you have ready a form or a critique on which to take notes, you have your ideas organized and many of your points already listed. Again, be certain you know exactly what the assignment includes. Are you merely to enjoy a good speech? Are you to make notes concerning your feelings during a speech? Are you to comment on the delivery of the speech? Are you to summarize the speech or make notes on the content of the speech? Are you to report on both the content and the delivery?

1. *Notes on Delivery.* If you have been asked to comment on the delivery of a speech, your notes should be prepared ahead of time with headings defining the things you are to observe. A good listening report should include generalizations *supported by reasons* or *evidence.* For example, do not report only that the speaker had poor posture; give evidence that he had poor posture. Did he have his weight distributed on only one foot? Did he shift his weight often? Did he lean on the speaker's stand? Did he have his hands in his pockets, behind his back, clasped in front of him? Give details and examples supporting the fact that the speaker had poor posture, or that he had good posture some of the time and bad posture most of the time. Include something concerning frequency. If a speaker shifted his weight two or three times during a speech, just mentioning this fact alone would seem to imply that he had poor posture when in truth he had good posture and the poor examples were exceptions. (For guidance you might use one of the listening sheets at the end of the book.)

2. *Notes on Content.* Note taking should reflect the fact that speeches are divided into introduction, body, and conclusion. Each of these divisions requires a particular kind of examination.

a. Introduction. Did the speaker have an obvious introduction or was it difficult to tell when the introduction stopped and the body began? Listen carefully for his opening statements. Were they attention getting? What method or methods did he use to get your attention? Did the speaker introduce his topic in his introduction? Generally or specifically? Did he include a transition into the body?

b. Body. Naturally, this division of the speech will produce the most complex notes. Although preliminary research will help you to understand the speech, your immediate responsibility is to listen carefully and to *take notes.* Some speeches are either so exciting or so boring that you will find you must discipline yourself to record comments.

Your method of taking notes will vary from speech to speech. Some speakers will keep their major points and their subpoints before their audiences at all times; they may introduce their statements with "My first point is . . ." or "My two reasons for feeling this way are. . . ." With signals such as these, you should have no difficulty outlining the speech. On the other hand, some speakers make it very difficult to take notes because they fail to organize what they say. Some speeches may be so difficult to outline that you may find it necessary to get the main ideas and to approximate subordinate ideas. One of the best ways to take notes for this type of speech is to leave plenty of space above and below any point that you record. You may find later that what you thought was a subordinate idea is really a main point or vice versa. In this way you can add above or below. Another way to take notes for a poorly organized speech is to draw a line down the middle of your page. At the left of the line, place what seems to be a major point or a generalization. At the right of the line, list facts, figures, and examples that seem to support or document the major points. Again, give yourself plenty of room above and below the points. Still another way to take notes is to try to follow the speech by the argument method; that is, make three columns on your page for main points, reasons for, and reasons against. When a speaker states what seems to be a major point, place it in the first column. If he supports the point with reasons or evidence, put that information in the second column. If he gives reasons or arguments against the point, place them in the third column.

You must be prepared to take notes in whatever seems to be the best method. Eventually you should experiment with several methods. The ultimate reason for taking notes is to use the information recorded. Evaluate your notes; if you find that they are ineffective, adjust your method.

Listen carefully for clues given by the speaker. Does he repeat important points? Does he summarize important points before he goes on to the next point? Does he include transitional sentences? Does he indicate the total number of points he has in mind? How many reasons? How many ways? Many times even a poorly organized speaker will make statements that will help you to organize your notes. It is also important to remember that even the poorest speech has something to offer every listener.

c. Conclusion. Does the speaker make it obvious that he is about to finish? Does he use the phrase "In conclusion" or "In summary"? Does he have a transition between the body and conclusion? Does he review his main points? Does he repeat the purpose of the speech? Does he make a concluding statement that makes it clear that he has ended his speech? Remember not to give just yes or no answers to the above questions. List examples used by the speaker.

SUMMARY

Listening is the comprehension and interpretation of what is heard. Effective listening demands deliberate concentration. Each listening experience must be approached with an open mind and with the proper attitude; preliminary research about the speaker and his topic will lead to greater understanding of the speech. The listener should make advance preparation for taking careful notes; a critique sheet or preliminary outline may help him.

To listen efficiently the listener must attempt to remain unbiased and not become emotionally involved in what the speaker is saying. In addition, the listener should listen analytically to both what is said and how it is said. Careful notes should be taken on the delivery of the speech and the content of the speech.

ASSIGNMENTS

1. On one of the Sundays during the first four weeks of the course, attend a church or synagogue. Make a list of emotional responses you had during the presentation, both affirmative and negative. Use the evaluation sheet at the end of the book as a guide.
2. During the middle weeks of the course, observe a guest speaker who speaks to a group outside the classroom. Using the evaluation sheet at the end of the book as a guide, make a listening report on the content of the speech.
3. Toward the last of the course, observe a guest speaker on campus or an off-campus speaker. Make a listening report on both the content and the delivery of the speech. The evaluation sheet at the end of the book may be used as a guide.

4. During the final round of speeches your instructor may assign each member of the class a listening assignment. Your instructor will designate a member of the class for each report, so that each class member will report on one other class member. Outline the speech during the delivery.
5. If possible, attend a debate on campus or one at a local high school. Make a listening report on the first affirmative speaker; outline the content of the speech, listing the proposition, the major points, and the arguments supporting the major points. Use the listening evaluation sheet at the end of the book as a guide. Review the information concerning outlining.
6. During the course your instructor may assign you a listening assignment for a lecture. You may be assigned to make a report during a lecture for another class or your instructor may ask you to outline one of his lectures. Review the information concerning outlining. Make an outline of a lecture for a single class period. Observe proper form.
7. During a TV or radio "talk" show, a debate, or an interview, select two or three major issues. List the issues and follow each with arguments in favor of the issue and arguments against the issue. Use the evaluation sheet at the end of the book as a guide.
8. Review the information concerning analytical listening. Analyze any speaker's supporting evidence. Make a list of emotional appeals made during the speech.

chapter seven
THE SPEECH TO INFORM

The speech to inform attempts to communicate with listeners in order to aid their understanding and to give information. The process of informing has increased in significance as our society has increased in size and complexity. Many businesses and professions now have special departments that exist only to inform the general public. Our government has established agencies to supply information to the public, nationally and internationally. Our entire educational system exists to pass information from instructor to student. Much of our time is spent either in conveying information or in receiving information.

The speaker must remember that communicating information to an audience can prove to be difficult. Any one group of listeners varies in the ability of the individuals within the group to understand, and in the amount of previous knowledge brought to the speaking situation. A speaker must attempt to communicate with as many of his listeners as possible. If he miscalculates the knowledge of his audience, he may soon lose their interest. People do not listen attentively to what they already know; neither can they follow what they do not understand. The entire informational process must be carefully thought out and organized, and the audience carefully analyzed.

There are four types of informative speeches to be considered in this chapter: the speech of introduction, the speech to demonstrate, the speech to instruct, and the speech to describe.

I. THE SPEECH OF INTRODUCTION

Your first speech will very likely be a speech of introduction. The purpose of the speech of introduction is to introduce yourself or another student to the class. The speech of introduction also serves to introduce you to speaking.

A. Self-Introduction

The speech of self-introduction should be the easiest speech to give because you are, in effect, an authority about yourself. This speech should include information that will tell your class and instructor what makes you what you are. It should include the important events that have influenced your life and that have helped to shape your personality. In many cases it means going back over your life carefully and organizing earlier events. Discussing the speech with those who know you can often be helpful.

Like all speeches, the introductory speech should have an interesting and attention-getting introduction. Do not begin by saying, "Today I am going to tell you about me." On the other hand, do not be overdramatic, as is the following example: "It was a dark rainy night. The moon was partly hidden by foreboding clouds. The silence of the house was disturbed by the clock striking four. Suddenly a man jumped up, dressed quickly, and drove his wife to the hospital at top speed. A few hours later I was born." Try not to be negative. Do not begin by saying, "I haven't done anything or gone any place" or "Nothing really important has ever happened to me." Try to be positive and, if possible, amusing in your introduction. You might start with an interesting incident that happened early in your life or an amusing anecdote that your parents enjoy telling about you. Be sure to give your name early in the introduction, so that your audience can associate your comments with you as a person.

The introductory speech can be organized in several ways. Review the rules of outlining and apply them carefully. Do not, as one student did, make your first major point "My Life." On the other hand, do not have a large number of main points. Statistics are not as important in this type of speech as in others. Giving your date of birth, your age, the number of brothers and sisters is not as enlightening as relating the important events in your life, your interests, your hobbies, your desires.

Do be factual. Do not make up events or interests just because you believe that your life is not interesting. The individual who thinks that his life is not interesting or that he has done nothing is an individual who is merely scratching the surface. Dig a little deeper. If you have not participated in sports or if you do not have hobbies or if you have not traveled, what have you done? Does your family like to do things together? Have you had interesting jobs? Have you fixed or made anything interesting? Have you met interesting people? Is there something you enjoy doing more than anything else? What do you do for fun? How do you occupy your spare time?

B. Introducing a Classmate

A variation of the introductory speech is to introduce a classmate. This may be done in one of two ways. Students may divide into groups of two, with each of the pair introducing the other; or each student may introduce the student next to him. To introduce another student, you must ask questions. This process of asking questions, termed interviewing, involves basic principles to be observed in this method of gathering information.

1. *Privacy.* Make suitable provisions for privacy during the interview. Those engaged in an interview can think and talk more efficiently if there are no disturbing influences.

2. *Preparation.* Find out as much as you can beforehand about the person whom you will interview. What do others know and think about him? What are his characteristics? Does he work? Does he have any hobbies or special interests? How does he spend his time? When you have asked questions of others, write out as many remaining questions as possible before the actual interview. Try to organize the questions into areas of interest so that questions are not repeated. However, you may choose to let circumstances determine the order and progress of the interview. Your purpose is to get the person to talk about himself. If one statement reminds him of something else, let him follow his own line of thought. You can organize your notes at a later time.

3. *Recording.* Ideally, the interview should be recorded on a tape recorder. If this is not possible, be certain to take very good notes. If you have written questions before the interview, leave plenty of space between the questions in which to record the answers during the interview. Try to organize your questions by topics (family, hobbies, sports, interests, jobs, to list just a few). If you are not certain of an answer, be sure to ask to have the answer repeated. An incorrect statement is worse than no statement at all. However, listen carefully and try to write the answer as the person states it. Do not abbreviate or take shortcuts unless you can use shorthand. Many times when an interviewer tries to read his notes at a later time, he

cannot make out what his notes say. For the same reason, write clearly and carefully.

4. Diplomacy. Remain patient, tactful, pleasant, and friendly throughout the interview. Avoid questions that are too personal or that the person being interviewed may not wish to answer. Do not repeat a question that he seems to be avoiding. Either reword the question or go on to another one.

When you have the information you need, organize the speech as you would any other speech. Be certain to mention the name of the individual in your introduction. It is a good idea to have the individual stand when you first mention his name. You may want to ask him to stand briefly just before you begin the introduction.

II. THE DEMONSTRATION SPEECH

The purpose of the demonstration, or how-to-do-it, speech is to inform by means of a demonstration. The test of a good demonstration speech is the results. Members of the audience should be sufficiently well informed by the demonstration so that they can perform the activity that was demonstrated. Since the demonstration explains how the steps of a certain operation lead to its completion, the correct order is usually of great importance. And just as a chain may fail because of a weak link, the demonstration speech may fail if any one point is unclear.

The process should be divided into a series of distinct steps. However, the step-by-step format may need to be interrupted by descriptions, definitions, or other explanatory asides. A generalized pattern might include the necessary materials, the steps of the process, a look at the completed project, and possibly a brief analysis of how it works. Words such as "when," "then," "after," "now," and "until" are used frequently in demonstration speeches. However, no single word should be overused.

A good outline, important in any speaking situation, is essential for a speech to demonstrate. If the steps are not in order, or if something has been left out, the demonstration will be a failure. A good test for the outline is to give it to a friend to see whether he can give the same demonstration using your outline.

Try to keep the subject simple enough to comply with the time limits, yet interesting enough to keep the audience's attention. Review the principles for using visual aids; they certainly apply to the demonstration speech.

There are several ways to demonstrate how to do something: by going through the actual process, by using a model, or by using progressive illustrations.

A. Actual Process

Some demonstrations lend themselves to completion during the actual speech. For instance, you can demonstrate the entire process of shining shoes, bandaging an arm, or cleaning a gun. If the process involves an activity, such as a swimming stroke, a wrestling hold, or tumbling, or if it should prove awkward to perform by yourself, as bandaging an arm would be, ask someone to assist you in your demonstration. However, be sure to ask your assistant before the time of the speech.

B. Using a Model

In some instances it would be impossible to bring the item being demonstrated into the room, or it might be difficult to do the actual demonstration in class. A student nurse who wants to demonstrate how to inject insulin might use an orange. A student who wants to demonstrate how to paint a car might bring a car model to class. A doll can be used to demonstrate how to change diapers or how to bathe a baby. Make certain that any problems that might occur in the real process are mentioned during a demonstration involving a model or substitution.

C. Using Progressive Illustrations

Some demonstrations would take too long to do during the time allotted for a classroom speech. This problem can be overcome by using either pictures or illustrations to demonstrate the progress from step to step. If you want to demonstrate how to develop a picture, you might prepare negatives to illustrate the various stages of development. During the demonstration, you would not actually do each step but would explain how each step is done and then show what the negative looks like at the end of each step; a completely developed picture should climax the process. Similarly, for a knitting demonstration an entire sweater could not be knit before the class; yet the various steps could be shown by the use of several partially knitted sweaters. Some oriental paper folding also takes a good deal of time. Rather than completing the entire process during the speech, a speaker could use partially completed examples or pictures or charts to show each step.

D. Types of Demonstration Speeches

Demonstration speeches seem to fall into several categories. In turn, the speeches themselves have somewhat similar internal divisions. Note the categories and divisions of the speech topics listed.

How to Play Games and Sports

How to play chess (the pieces, the moves, the object)
How to play bridge (the cards, the rules, the scoring)
How to play golf (wood shots, iron shots, putting)
How to snow ski (starting, going downhill, stopping)
How to bowl (the equipment, the fingering, the approach, the release)

How to Play a Musical Instrument

How to play drums (equipment, sticks, brushes, pedal)
How to play the clarinet (assembling, fingering, blowing)
How to play the guitar (tuning, fingering, picking)
How to play the piano (posture, the hands, the feet)
How to play the harmonica (the lips, the tongue, the hands)

How to Use Something

How to use an iron (equipment, techniques, special areas)
How to use a tape recorder (operation, recording, listening)
How to use a gun (loading, aiming, shooting)
How to use a record (handling, cleaning, playing)
How to use makeup (foundation, eyes, cheeks, lips)

How to Make Something

How to make paper flowers (materials, folding paper, finishing paper)
How to make a rag angel (wire frame, body, head, arms and legs)
How to mat a picture (preparing the picture, the mat, fastening)
How to carve leather (equipment, pattern, steps)
How to cover a book (cutting, folding, pasting)

The listed topics are only to give an idea of what can be done and how certain divisions within the speeches seem to be natural divisions. Remember, originality is important when choosing a subject.

III. THE INSTRUCTIONAL SPEECH

The instructional speech provides information of an educational nature; that is, information that increases knowledge and understanding. Its purpose is not to influence or to persuade but simply to inform in order to broaden knowledge. The speaker actually teaches a miniature lesson.

For this type of speaking it is essential that the topic chosen be specific and limited in scope. A student could very well select a topic from his major or minor fields or from current events. Although visual aids are not absolutely necessary for this type of speech, they are an advantage; it is always easier for an audience to visualize the operation of a machine or the field of battle if pictures or diagrams are used.

Most subjects for instructional speeches fall into one of two types: historical subjects, usually presented chronologically, and analytical subjects, usually presented by means of functional analysis.

A. Historical Subjects

Historical instructional speeches are concerned with topics that describe what has happened in the past, the way something is now, or a combination of the two. An instructional speech never projects into the future; it is concerned only with the past and the present. Titles using such beginnings as "The History of," "The Life of," "The Story of," "The Study of" are often found. Usually, but not always, a chronological method of organization is used. A speech concerned with the development of the atomic bomb would probably include a chronological, step-by-step, development. If you were to choose the life of Everett Dirksen as a topic, you might want to use the order of early life, middle life, and later life; or you might want to discuss Dirksen as a political speaker, a legal speaker, and a public speaker. Your time limit, your audience, and your own interests should guide you in choosing a specific topic.

B. Analytical Subjects

An analytical instructional speech explains and analyzes how the parts of something relate to each other and what function each performs. The first step in preparing an analytical speech is to determine a clear basis of division. The entire unit must be regarded as constituted of its parts. The second step is to determine the exact function and interworkings of each part. Some topics are more difficult than others because several things occur simultaneously. For example, an explanation of how a gasoline engine operates must include a step-by-step process and at the same time express the interacting relationships. The organization of the speech into stages as subdivisions would help clarify the process for the audience.

To illustrate the difference between a speech to demonstrate and a speech to instruct, the following example may help. A student interested in a gasoline engine might demonstrate how to ring a piston for his demonstration speech. Another time he might inform and instruct the class with a speech on how the piston operates during combustion. Both speeches are concerned with pistons, but each has a different basic purpose. Different interests in a subject will also lead to different approaches to the subject. The automobile lends itself to many varied subjects for analytical speeches. Again, time is an important element; there must be enough time to explain how an entire process works. There may be enough time to explain how an entire motor works, or there may only be enough time to explain how a piston works. Be sure you know the time limits you have been assigned, and be sure to practice your speech so that you know that it fits within the time limits.

C. Suggestions for Instructional Speeches

The following is a sample list of possible instructional speeches.

Historical

the "New Left"	trading stamps	the United Nations
gunpowder	rockets	modern art
the knife	radio	the chair
the postage stamp	television	paper
basketball	flying	modern plumbing
football	electricity	maps

the life of

the bee	Everett Dirksen	a drug addict
the ant	Dick Gregory	an alcoholic
the wasp	John F. Kennedy	a deaf-mute
tropical fish	Helen Keller	an orphan
a dog	Martin Luther King	a flower child

the study of

the zodiac	cancer	hypnotism
astrology	advertising	TV commercials
E.S.P.	crime	gambling
magic	the stock market	politics
dreams	evolution	color

Analytical

How we speak	How digestion works
How we breathe	How radar works
How cancer kills	How the mind works
How drugs destroy	How jet propulsion works
How electricity works	The operation of the gasoline engine

IV. THE DESCRIPTIVE SPEECH

The aim of the speech to describe is to make the audience see with a certain amount of detail what has produced an impression upon the speaker. The purpose of this speech is to develop your natural instinct for observing the world around you and for communicating your observations and experiences to others. This type of speech is beneficial in many ways. It requires the speaker to observe carefully, to organize well, and to use descriptive language. Like the blind men describing the elephant, if a complete picture is not given, a distorted view will be the result.

If the listener is to gain a mental picture of what the speaker describes, the speaker must organize and unify his description in some way. He should make clear the physical point of view from which he describes his subject. By limiting his account to what he could see from his vantage point, the speaker not only provides organization but suggests credibility and naturalness. In addition, the speaker should consider the scale or size upon which the description is made. Minute details should not be included if the speaker's point of view is some distance from the object. The speaker should set a scale and remain consistent with details throughout the description. However, scale changes could very well be included if this is part of the organizational plan and if the changes are made obvious to the listeners. For example, you might describe the St. Louis Gateway Arch from a great distance, move to the foot of it for further description, and take a final vantage point from the observation deck inside the arch. Any change in direction or scale should progress according to some pattern made clear to your audience; for example, you may want to follow the course of a river, the direction of weather belts, the landing patterns at an airport, or a painting from focal point to dim periphery.

There are two types of descriptive speeches: objective and subjective. Objective description is the description of the scientist. Subjective description is the description of the artist.

A. Objective Description

Objective description is impersonal and technical; its primary purpose is to present detail concerning the appearance or characteristics of a person, place, or object. The speaker attempts to describe what has been before him, what he has literally seen, what any impartial, impersonal observer would have seen. Like a scientist, the speaker bases an objective description on technical facts. What is described can be checked and verified—it is directed to the understanding. Objective description calls for two things: a detailed study of what is actually there, and a careful choice of words to convey as concretely as possible what is seen. The objective description tends to be enumerative.

One of the main problems in giving objective description is that the speech may end up a catalog of unrelated details or particulars. Although each part or section or area should be recorded with precision and accuracy, it is important that the parts be related in such a way that the audience can visualize the subject as an entire unit.

B. Subjective Description

The purpose of subjective description is to give a very personal description. The subject of the description will be influenced by the feelings that were aroused in the speaker and the impressions that were made on him. The technical facts are not ignored, but they are used only to aid the speaker in re-creating his initial dominant impression. Thus, subjective description tends to be selective and impressionistic. The speaker's aim is to give his audience an experience by means of imagination, to convey the sense of living reality. He is concerned with particulars as they occur to him—particular experiences and particular objects. Such a description is an appeal to the senses and to the emotions. Details should be presented in such a way that the listeners share the speaker's emotions. Subjective description should not be confined to the visual detail; any sensory detail (the senses of sound, smell, and possibly taste) that seems to enhance the vividness of the subject should be used.

C. Suggestions for Descriptive Speeches

Many of the topics listed below lend themselves to either objective or subjective description. Your first step would be to decide whether you would rather be objective or subjective.

Describe

- a newborn baby
- your favorite painting
- a busy intersection
- a small town
- the first snow
- a sunset (or sunrise)
- the face of an old man
- the side of a mountain
- a puppy
- a Picasso sculpture
- a near accident
- your first attempt to ski
- sailing
- flying or gliding
- seeing for the first time:
  - Niagara Falls
  - Williamsburg
  - Statue of Liberty
  - Grand Canyon
  - U.S. Capitol

SUMMARY

The purpose of the speech to inform is to give information and to aid in understanding. The speaker estimates the knowledge of his audience in order to communicate with all who hear him. His ideas must be presented in an orderly manner, and the order of presentation must be made clear to his audience.

The four types of informative speeches are the speech to introduce, the speech to demonstrate, the speech to instruct, and the speech to describe. When the speaker introduces himself, he includes the details that have had special influence in his life; he is neither overdramatic nor apologetic but is positive and factual. If he introduces another, he applies the proper guides to gather information: interview in private, be well prepared, record correctly, and be diplomatic. A demonstration speech should result in the listeners' learning how to do something. A demonstration might utilize the actual process, a model, or a series of progressive illustrations. An instructional speech is designed to increase knowledge; these speeches are either historical or analytical. The descriptive speech involves either objective or subjective description. The description should be either factual and scientific, or personal and impressionistic.

ASSIGNMENTS

For the following speaking assignments prepare an outline and present the outline to your instructor just prior to your speaking.

1. Introductory Speech. The instructor will inform you whether your speech is to be self-introductory or whether you are to introduce someone else in class. Review the information on speeches to introduce and on outlining. Time: 4-6 minutes.
2. Demonstration Speech. Review the information on demonstration speeches and on the use of visual aids. Present the speech using actual process, a model, or progressive illustrations. Time: 5-7 minutes.
3. Instructional Speech. Review the information on instructional speeches. Present a historical or an analytical instructional speech. Feel free to use visual aids to help illustrate your speech. Time: 5-7 minutes.
4. Descriptive Speech. Review the information on descriptive speeches. Present an objective or a subjective descriptive speech. Do *not* use visual aids for this speech. Time: 5-7 minutes.

chapter eight
THE SPEECH TO ENTERTAIN

The speech to entertain is communication for the purpose of enjoyment. At times an audience wants to listen to presentations for which the basic purpose is neither to inform nor to persuade. Although some of the subjects used for speeches to entertain may include material to inform and/or persuade, the basic purpose of a speech to entertain is to provide a pleasurable diversion for those listening. Speeches to entertain generally fall into two classes: interpretation of the written word and after-dinner speeches.

I. INTERPRETATION

From the time man first communicated with his fellowman, the interpreter has been listened to with interest and with pleasure. Modern interpreters range from the elementary classroom teacher or librarian, who must captivate children with a literary selection, to the author who reads his own work during a professional appearance from the lecture platform, on stage, or on television. More and more people are finding enjoyment in reading aloud and in hearing someone else read aloud. In coffee houses or wherever students gather, there is an increasing demand for interpretation of original works or the works of others in what is usually an informal situation.

Interpretation is the art of translation. Written symbols are translated into thoughts and feelings. The interpretive speaker attempts to communicate emotional experiences to his audience. If he is successful, his audience not only gains pleasure from the translation but actually participates as well. Thus, there must be communication from writer to interpreter to audience. The importance of communication is essentially doubled in the art of interpretation.

In interpretation, which is a rather unique speaking situation, the emphasis is on the delivery of the material. You will find that interpretation is an excellent exercise to improve vocal delivery, posture, gestures, speaker-audience relationship, and poise. Because you have your material with you and you are actually "reading" from the printed page, there is less tendency to have stage fright. At the same time, since the speech itself is already prepared, you have more time to practice your speech and to work on the physical delivery. In addition, the emphasis on vocal delivery will help you to improve your articulation, pronunciation, and vocal variety.

If you are to interpret effectively, you must first carefully choose the material you will interpret, understand the material, prepare the material for reading, and practice reading the material aloud.

A. Choosing the Material

The first step in selecting material is to read. Many books in every library are devoted to material that lends itself to interpretation. Many magazines include poems and short stories that read well aloud. Do not choose selections only because they are well known and often used by others. However, you should choose only material which has intrinsic qualities of good style.

Find several selections that appeal to you. Locate material that means something to you, that expresses what you would like to say the way you would like to say it—outstanding material that causes you to thrill, to "tingle" as you read it for the first time. When you have located several selections that you appreciate, try reading them aloud. Keep in mind the fact that some selections can be read well by one individual but not by another. Find selections that "fit" you. That is to say, selections that *you* can read easily, selections in which the phrasing seems to fall naturally for you. Avoid selections that are difficult for you to read aloud, selections that include words difficult for you to say or phrases and sentences difficult to read.

When you have found selections that seem to say what you want to say and in the way that you would like to say it, then consider your audience. Not only should you be able to appreciate the material that you have chosen, but your audience should also be able to appreciate it. Do not choose material that would be offensive to your audience, for your purpose is to entertain. As with any material, keep in mind the age and background of your audience. If your audience is made up of people your own age, the chances are they will enjoy the same material that you enjoy. You must carefully evaluate the work: "Is my material in good taste?" "Does it have literary value?" "Will my audience enjoy it?" "Will my audience be stimulated?"

B. Understanding the Material

You must understand what you are reading in order to communicate effectively with your audience. To successfully interpret the works of another, you must know something about both the writer and the selection.

1. *The Author.* Many times it is helpful to know important facts concerning the author. Statistical data concerning the writer is generally less useful than information about the writer's philosophy of life, his reasons for writing, and his mood at the time of writing. The period during which an author wrote often has influence on the work; for example, the Gold Rush days, the Roaring Twenties, the years of any war or depression, and certainly the present period are influences on the writing of specific periods. A young writer sees the world in a different way from that in which he sees it later. Knowing such things about the writer will help you to understand what he is trying to say and why he wants to say it.

2. *The Material.* What do the words mean? Although an assignment to read a short selection and to know what it means sounds elementary, it may not be as easy as it seems. To interpret material effectively you must know *all* the meanings, not just the obvious meaning. Does the writer mean only what is obvious, or are there hidden meanings? Are his words to be taken literally or figuratively? Do you understand the connotative and denotative meanings? Are there explicit and implicit meanings? Are there allusions or symbolic meanings? Answers to these questions are prerequisites to understanding and interpreting effectively.

You should enjoy reading the work for the first time. After one careful reading the obvious or explicit meaning should be clear; you should be able to determine the author's theme. In a sentence or two write out what the author was trying to say. This must be the first step. In many cases the writer has a deeper meaning that he is trying to express. The reader must attempt to determine the implicit meaning if there is one. In some cases, the entire selection may be symbolic or allegorical.

The second step is to read the material a second time and to note any words or expressions that you do not understand. Use a dictionary to check these words for both meaning and pronunciation. In addition to the dictionary definition, you must also know the author's intention if you are to interpret his work properly. Authors often write with shades of inference, implied conclusions, and connotative meanings. Remember also that some writers, especially poets, are attempting to communicate chiefly emotion. Take into consideration the fact that critics often disagree about the meaning of certain words in many selections. The important point to remember is that you must have some reason for interpreting as you do. You must be able to defend your interpretation.

The third reading of the selection should be for the purpose of determining the author's structure. Read to discover the way in which the author organizes his ideas. How does he develop his theme? Where are his climaxes? What is the major climax? What are his thought patterns?

C. Preparing the Material

When you feel that you have determined what the author was trying to say, then you are ready to prepare the material in such a way that you can easily express the meanings, emotions, and thoughts to your audience.

Read the selection aloud in order to concentrate first on phrasing and then on emphasis. Naturally the phrasing must be smooth. Short, jerky phrases are just as bad as long, drawn-out phrases. The interpreter must always remember that he must make the punctuation clear with his voice, because the audience cannot see the punctuation. Phrasing usually depends upon three things: the writer's punctuation, the rhythm of the selection, and the interpreter's breathing. Look first at the punctuation. A long sentence is usually divided by commas and other punctuation marks. Do these breaks and pauses lend themselves to meaningful phrasing? Do the word-group arrangements create rhythmic patterns? The rhythm of poetry is usually much more obvious than that of prose. Finally, do the previously determined steps allow for an easy breathing pattern, or do you find yourself running out of breath or speeding up your tempo? If you sound breathy, or if you run out of breath, you will have to rework the phrasing. The interpreter not only pauses for emphasis; he must pause to breathe as well. Whenever your breathing is obvious, the pattern is poor. All three, punctuation, rhythm, and your breathing, must work together. The phrasing must be perfected to allow the interpreter to breathe easily and naturally, to show the meaning of the phrase, and to maintain the natural rhythm of the selection.

When you have determined the phrasing, you must then concentrate on the emphasis within the phrases. Remember that interpretation is not simply the reading of words. The emotions, meanings, and thoughts of words and phrases must be expressed by changes in the voice. To fail to emphasize is to be monotonous; to emphasize to extreme is to defeat the purpose. Vocal variety is important in all speech activities; it is essential in interpretation to express meanings and emotions. Changes in pitch, volume, and rate, which contribute to the vocal variety of interpretation, should be indicated in the script.

1. *Pitch.* Changes in pitch, the tone level of the voice, express overall moods as well as emotions. A high pitch expresses both joy and anger. A low pitch expresses sadness as well as sincerity. Pitch changes between words are called steps, and those within words or syllables are called slides. Slides may be upward slides, downward slides, or slides that begin upward, reach a high point, and go downward. For example, applying all three slides, one at a time, to the word *Oh* gives three entirely different meanings. Experiment with using pitch in various ways until you are satisfied with the result.

2. *Volume and Rate.* Volume and rate often work together in interpretation. When the interpreter builds toward a climax, he usually increases both the speed and volume from phrase to phrase, sentence to sentence, until he reaches the climax. Usually there is a pause following the climax to let the audience relax and to let them feel the full extent of the emotion just expressed. Pauses are essential to interpretation. Always remember that an audience must be *guided.* A pause in the wrong place can change the entire meaning of what is being expressed. Pauses are also used to build suspense and to reinforce an idea. When you pause after an important idea, the idea has a tendency to repeat itself, again and again, in the minds of the audience. Changes in rate are also used to indicate changes in emotions or thoughts. An increase in rate can show excitement or eagerness; a slowness of rate can show calmness, sadness, or deliberateness.

3. *The Script.* Once the phrasing and emphasis have been determined, the interpreter should prepare his script so that it can be easily read. All material to be used should be typed or carefully printed with at least one full space between lines of material. Use only one side of the paper. Place the pages in a large loose-leaf notebook in which they will turn easily and noiselessly.

The script should be marked so that the correct emphasis and phrasing can be repeated. Everyone must determine which one of the various systems of marking is best for him. To show phrasing, some get along very well with ordinary punctuation. Others prefer to use a single vertical line (|) for a short pause and a double vertical line (||) for long pauses. Still others indicate phrasing with spaces, using single or multiple spaces between phrases or placing each phrase on a separate line. Upward slides can be shown by placing an upward-slanting line (/), downward slides by a line slanting downward (\), and multiple slides by a combination of these lines (/\). Steps can be shown by placing the words on different levels. Stress or emphasis can be shown by marking directly under the words or syllables to be stressed. A heavy line, a double line, or a colored line can be used for primary stress; a thin line, a single line, or a wavy line can be used for secondary stress. General volume changes can be shown by two converging or diverging lines (> <). Rate changes can be shown by using a single line under the phrase or sentences, with arrow marks along the line to show an increase or decrease in speed (>> >>> > > > > > >>>> > >>). These are just a few of the many mechanical methods that are used to mark a script.

4. The Program Script. With either a single selection or with several selections, a good introduction is essential. Like all introductions, it must get the audience's attention, establish rapport, and give some idea of what is to follow. The introduction should serve to get the audience in the correct mood and to introduce the theme of the work or works selected. In many cases it is necessary to say something about the author or authors. Unless the theme is a somber one, such as war or death, it is often advantageous to include some humor in the introduction. In some instances a very short selection or excerpt can be included as part of the introduction. This often says more about the author, the mood, and the theme than many words by the interpreter.

Transitions are essential to a presentation involving more than one selection. The transition between selections must maintain the mood of the last selection and at the same time introduce the next selection. The transition must be brief and to the point. In some instances a phrase from the one selection can be related to the next. The transition also gives the audience time to relax if the emotion has been intense.

In some instances a conclusion is necessary to actually conclude. That is to say, the audience may need a few additional remarks to know that the program is over. The speaker may conclude, for instance, by saying a few words about the theme, by repeating a few key words from the material, or by generalizing about what has been interpreted. In many instances, no conclusion is necessary. The interpreter may have built his program so that the concluding selection acts as a conclusion for the program; in this case additional comments might destroy the mood.

The introduction, the transitions, and the conclusion may also be parts of the interpreter's script. These should be typed out, properly spaced and marked, and inserted in the proper positions as part of the program script. Time should never be wasted. Whatever the interpreter says should be necessary and should provide a bond between the interpreter and his audience and the audience and the material.

D. Delivering the Material

In any speaking assignment the delivery of the material is as important as the material itself. In interpretation, the delivery is actually more important. You must deliver the material in such a way that the audience is able to imagine and to picture the emotions, attitudes, and actions suggested by the words. The interpreter suggests by means of voice, gestures, and movements; the audience imagines.

1. The Voice. Your voice must carry both thought and emotion to your audience. Pauses, emphases, rate changes, volume changes are all extremely important to convey meanings to your audience. It is essential that you deliver your material with smoothness and polish. Hesitant delivery, vocalized pauses, incorrect pronunciations, improper emphasis will all have a tendency to destroy the communications between you and your audience. To accomplish effective delivery, you must prepare adequately and then practice your speech several times.

2. *Gestures.* Gestures are usually limited during interpretation, because the script is usually held during the presentation. It is suggested that you hold the material in one hand and use the other to follow the script or to make gestures. Hold the script as steadily as possible, for moving it is a distraction that tends to destroy the mood. Hold the script in such a way that you can read it easily; do not let it block your face from the audience. The position of the script must be comfortable to you; the best distance is usually midway between the waist and the eyes. Hand and arm gestures should be used with moderation.

In interpretation, facial expressions are far more important than gestures. The audience should see the speaker's face and eyes as much as possible. Although you are "reading" your material, you should be familiar enough with it to the extent that you can look up *at least* as much as you look down. With practice you will find that you need to look down for only a glance to see several sentences. Facial expressions should be natural and should express what is said. If the interpreter truly understands what he is interpreting, facial expressions will "come from the inside." It is mainly with the face that the interpreter establishes empathy and shows emotion. If you smile, your audience will feel like smiling; if you frown, your audience will feel like frowning as well. If you can truly respond to what you are reading, you can expect the audience to respond to you.

3. *Movement.* As with gestures, movement must by necessity be curtailed during interpretation. Even though the material being read may call for movement, you are not expected to move in such a situation; at most, slight bodily movements can be used to suggest emotions or greater movements. However, you may want to move to make transitions. When you finish a selection and take a step or two as a physical transition, the members of the audience also feel that they can move a little and get settled for the next selection. Movement should always be purposeful and in moderation during interpretation. Excessive movement distracts during any speech; it destroys the mood during interpretation.

II. AFTER-DINNER SPEAKING

After-dinner speeches have come to be a traditional form of entertainment. Most organizations have each year at least one banquet featuring a guest speaker. The warm, friendly atmosphere of an after-dinner situation lends itself to an entertaining speech.

It is essential that an after-dinner speech be appropriate for the occasion. Although humor is an essential part of an after-dinner speech, the speech should include a message over and above the humor. The speech may be a tribute to a sentiment, an ideal, an activity, an object, an individual, or a group. Ideally, the subject should be light enough to be enjoyable, yet serious enough to give the audience something to think about. Topics such as leadership, kindness, faithfulness, life, love, fatherhood, and good sportsmanship lend themselves to an after-dinner speaking situation.

A. Construction

The introduction of an after-dinner speech must be given special attention. The introduction sets the mood for the remainder of the speech. It is important to make the audience feel relaxed and at ease. Such an introduction often takes longer to deliver than that of any other speech. The chances are that those in the group will have some common interests, such as those based on club membership, patronage, religious affiliation, or civic responsibility. By making reference to your audience's common interest and experiences, you can begin to establish rapport with the audience. In the introduction you should also take time to mention any relationship that you might have with the group, either by affiliation or experience. The introduction must set forth the subject of the speech in such a way that you retain the attention gained with light preliminary remarks.

The body of the speech should be developed according to a specific and obvious plan. Feel free to mention the major points to be presented and to repeat each point as it is developed. Name the five elements of leadership, the four kinds of love, the three types of fatherhood. The major points should be developed to a large degree by stories, anecdotes, illustrations, word pictures, and personal experiences; however, make clear to what point each of these relates. Statistics and documentation are not usually part of an after-dinner speech, for this speech is basically an appeal to the emotions.

In the conclusion the major points of the speech should be repeated and climaxed with a thought or an idea that will leave the audience with something to think on. A good closing for an after-dinner speech might very well include a quotation, a selection of poetry, or a personal story that sums up what you have been attempting to say.

B. Humor

Some people feel that they just cannot tell a joke. The fact is that they just do not know *how* to be humorous. To make an audience laugh, a speaker must have the proper material, must be aware of the basic rules of humor, and must have experience.

1. Gathering Material. There are many sources for humorous stories, quips, jokes, anecdotes, and quotations. Students assigned an after-dinner speech often go to the library to look for several "joke" books, collections of so-called humorous stories and jokes arranged by topics. The irony of such a move is that very few entries in such a collection are usable in the context of a particular speech. Magazines such as the *Reader's Digest* are good sources of humor; however, a large majority of any audience will have read the same magazines. For the same reason, popular stories that are making the rounds should be avoided. If such sources of humor are inadequate, you may very well wonder where you should turn for humorous material. To find the answer, you must first realize what makes people laugh.

All humor can be traced back to seven or so basic themes. Although stories may seem new, they are actually variations on basic themes. Psychologists often give long and elaborate explanations of why people laugh. However, people generally laugh because what they hear or see is either incongruous or unexpected. Incongruity consists of statements or acts that, in a nice way, are inconsistent, unsuitable, or inappropriate. Something is unexpected when it is different from what is expected. Both the incongruous and the unexpected can be observed on the streets, on campus, at home, any place. The best humor may be simply telling what you have seen or heard. Fashions are often sources of humor. Comments by children are often very funny. Embarrassing situations in which you have found yourself may become funny with time.

When you come upon something humorous in a book or from observation, write it down on a note card; for although you may think that a story is so good that you could not possibly forget it, the chances are that you will. Do not overlook the fact that humor is versatile: a single humorous incident can lend itself to many subjects by adaptation—by changing profession, location, or identity. Humor is all around; record and adapt it.

2. Basic Rules of Humor. Humor can be very tricky. The teller of jokes and stories must be very careful in selecting his material and in presenting it.

a. Material. Above all, be certain that the humor used illustrates or illuminates the point being made. Do not use material that might embarrass anyone present. You should check with an individual if you are going to use his name or tell a story about him. If you are telling a story about yourself, neither belittle yourself nor embarrass your family. Although it will be obvious to most of those present that you are stretching the truth somewhat from time to time, there are always a few who will believe everything you say.

Avoid private or "inside" jokes. Avoid jokes with excessive profanity. Avoid "I said, then he said" stories. Avoid dialect jokes unless you are a member of the group. Avoid using too many puns. A few good "groaners" are fine; however, remember that the pun *is* the lowest form of humor. Avoid such trite expressions as "A funny thing happened to me tonight" or "The other day" or "On the way here" or "That reminds me of a joke."

Above all, plan ahead. Be certain of your wording. A wrong word or a forgotten word can destroy the humor. The order of telling a story is important. The laugh-provoking line is usually the final line, and the key words are usually toward the end of the last line. You may want to write out key phrases and especially the punch lines of any stories you tell.

b. Delivery. Many speakers believe that a funny story will tell itself, that simply repeating what seemed funny to them is enough; they could not be more wrong. If a humorous story is delivered without enthusiasm, without animation, it will most certainly fall flat. If the speaker does not seem to be enjoying himself, if he does not have a twinkle in his eye and a smile about his lips, the audience may not realize that he is telling something funny. An audience must be led and must be "told" when to laugh. Remember that individuals in an audience will seldom laugh alone for fear that they are laughing at the wrong thing. A gesture, a facial expression, or both can be used to point out the exact time to laugh. On the other hand, do not laugh at your own jokes. Most good after-dinner speakers deliver their humor with no more than a broad smile. The speaker must avoid loud laughter.

Humor must be properly timed. The speaker must "build" toward his humorous climax; he must "point" the punch line. The rate of delivery usually picks up as the story or joke reaches its climax; this may also be true of volume. The voice must point out that the climax is coming. The speaker must also learn to "hold for laughs," that is, to pause for a very short time in order to allow the audience time to laugh. If he begins to talk again too soon, the laughter will die prematurely so that the members of the audience can hear what he has to say next. This is frustrating to an audience; people may not be so quick to laugh the next time for fear of missing something. Give the audience time to laugh and then begin to speak again just before the laughter dies entirely away.

If the audience does not laugh at your jokes or humorous stories, do *not* attempt to make a humorous recovery. If only a few members of the audience laugh, do not say something like "Thank you, relatives" or "At least I have a few friends here tonight." Do not try to recover by saying "It was funny when I told it to my mother" or "My neighbor thought it was funny." The best thing to do is to drop the humor at this point and go immediately into a more serious part of your speech. You may want to moderate your humorous elements somewhat. However, the chances are good that the audience will laugh the next time you illustrate a point with humor.

Speaker-audience relationship is essential to all speaking. It is difficult to make people laugh unless you deliver your material *to* them. Try to know your humorous stories well enough so that you can tell them while looking at your audience rather than reading from notes. Nothing destroys rapport with an audience as much as reading a speech.

3. Experience. It is only through practice that proper timing, proper emphasis, and proper bodily action can be achieved. Try to give your after-dinner speech to as many people as possible, your parents, your friends, your neighbors. Make certain that your speech meets the time requirements, for an after-dinner speaker may easily lose track of time.

SUMMARY

A speech to entertain is a speech to interpret a written selection or a speech given "after dinner." Both types should provide pleasurable diversion for the audience.

Interpretation is the art of translating written symbols into thoughts and feelings. The interpreter should choose a selection that has good style; the selection should inspire him and have value for his audience. The act of interpretation requires a thorough understanding of the material, research concerning the philosophy and background of the author, and a careful analysis of the theme and style of the material. Because interpretation requires that the voice express both thought and emotion by use of pauses, emphases, and changes in rate and volume, the interpreter should experiment with aspects of vocal delivery. He should mark a script with symbols to indicate phrases, emphases, and changes in volume and rate. The script should also include an introduction that sets the mood and introduces the theme of the work. Facial expressions used during interpretation should be natural and should reflect what is being read. Gestures and movements should be used with moderation. Interpretation must be a sincere presentation of the interpreter's understanding of what the author has written. There must be communication between the writer and the interpreter and between the interpreter and his audience.

The after-dinner speech must fit the speaker, the audience, and the occasion. The introduction must set the mood and make the audience feel at ease. It should include an idea of the more serious nature of the speech as well as humor. The body of the after-dinner speech should include an obvious plan developed by major points. These points should be supported by stories, anecdotes, illustrations, word pictures, and personal experiences. The conclusion should present a worthwhile thought.

The humor for an after-dinner speech should be gathered carefully from books, magazines, and personal experiences. The humorous material, carefully selected for pertinence and effect, should be delivered with enthusiasm; it should be properly timed and should be directed *to* the audience.

The ability to entertain is a challenging art. It requires a careful selection of material, a sensitive evaluation of the audience, and special attention to delivery.

ASSIGNMENTS

1. Prepare a single poem for interpretation. The introduction should include background information concerning the author, a general idea of the poem, and your reasons for selecting this particular poem. Time: 3-5 minutes.
2. Prepare a poem and a prose selection which have a common theme. The introduction should include information about the author, your theme idea, and your reasons for selection. Be certain to include a transition uniting the two selections. Include a conclusion if you feel that it is necessary. Time: 4-8 minutes.
3. Prepare a program script. Include a poem, a prose selection, and the climactic selection from a short story, a book, or a speech from a play. Be certain that all three selections have a common theme. Cut any selections necessary to balance the three, so that about equal time is spent on each. Include an effective introduction, workable transitions, and a conclusion if necessary. Review the information about the program script. Time: 6-10 minutes.

For the following speeches prepare an outline and present the outline to your instructor just prior to your speaking.

4. Prepare an after-dinner speech for an occasion for which you might reasonably be asked to speak. Be certain your introduction sets the scene and mentions why you have been chosen as guest speaker. Time: 6-8 minutes.
5. Prepare an after-dinner speech for an occasion in which you would not likely find yourself. Assume any character speaking at any banquet situation—for example, the guest speaker at a gourmet club or a world traveler at a travelers' club. Time: 6-8 minutes.

chapter nine

THE SPEECH TO PERSUADE

The Latin word *persuadere* means "to bring over by talking." In a speech to persuade, the speaker attempts to induce his audience to think or act in a certain way. Speeches to persuade are universally heard at all levels of communication; they are delivered by government officials, politicians, parents, teachers, and students. However, a speaker can effect persuasion only when an audience is not committed to the issue or when the audience professes the opposing side of the issue; otherwise the speaker merely reinforces what he and his audience already believe. Also, members of the audience must be free to think for themselves; otherwise the speaking situation is not conducive to persuasion.

The speaker attempts to persuade by inspiring trust and confidence, by appealing to emotions, and by using logical arguments. Aristotle called these three *ethos*, *pathos*, and *logos:* personal appeal, psychological appeal, and logical appeal. A speaker uses these appeals to try to influence the *convictions* or *beliefs* of others in *a speech to convince;* he uses them to influence the *actions* or *behavior* of others in *a speech to motivate.* Although the two types of speeches are similar in that both use all three types of appeals, their basic purposes vary to such a degree that they can be looked upon as different types of speeches. An understanding of the methods of persuasion is fundamental to both speeches to convince and speeches to motivate.

I. METHODS OF PERSUASION

Persuasion is not an end in itself; it is rather a method by which to reach an end. This method can be divided into ethical appeal, pathetic appeal, and logical appeal: *ethos*, *pathos*, and *logos.*

A. Ethos

Ethical appeal is personal persuasion. The speaker who has concern for his audience and who evokes confidence and trust has ethical appeal. A speaker's capacity for personal persuasion is based on his reputation, his appearance, what he says, and how he says it.

1. Reputation. Audiences may be asked to believe that something is true simply because someone in a responsible position says that it is true. A member of the FBI, Congress, or the Supreme Court is expected to be honest and to make rational statements. Often listeners are asked to accept such statements at face value without questioning the facts or logic behind the statements. In effect, it is the speaker's reputation that persuades. People believe what is said simply because they trust the individual speaker. If a speaker is known to be honest, fair, and trustworthy, if he holds a responsible position, if he is sufficiently educated, if he is a good husband and father, he has more ethical appeal than an individual who is known to be dishonest, uneducated, and unemployed, and who beats his wife and children. It is not always true that the individual who has a fine reputation is telling the truth or that a disreputable man is necessarily lying, but a good reputation is a valuable beginning for persuasion. In the classroom, a student's reputation will depend largely upon the work he does. If his speeches show that he has done adequate research, has organized his ideas carefully, and has perfected delivery, these attributes may help to establish *ethos.*

2. Appearance. An appropriate appearance enhances the personal appeal of a speaker. Do not misconstrue appropriate appearance to mean that you cannot dress informally; for example, in an informal speaking situation a speaker may choose to dress informally in an attempt to appear as one of the audience. On the other hand, most speaking situations imply that a speaker should be conservatively dressed. A slovenly, unclean speaker usually gives the audience the bias that his speech will have the same attributes.

3. Content. A persuasive speaker should make every attempt to establish *ethos* by what he says: establish common ground and identify with the audience, establish the fact that you are concerned for their welfare, and modestly establish your qualifications to speak on the subject. At times the common ground or the identification that you have with your audience is obvious. If you are speaking to a group of students, your status as a student is common to them; that fact may be important, especially if you are speaking about student affairs or problems. At other times, the common ground is not as obvious. You may find that the only thing you have in common with your audience is nationality. However, the fact that the proposition is important to everyone in the country is broad common ground. By pointing out to the audience that the problem affects them directly or that the solution would improve the situation for them specifically, you can help establish *ethos.* If you have had experiences that qualify you to speak on the topic, mention them in a modest way to enhance your *ethos.* However, do not exaggerate, generalize, or provoke. If you alienate your audience by what you say, you decrease your potential for ethical appeal.

4. Delivery. Because sincerity is an extremely important aspect of emotional appeal, the speaker should attempt to make his delivery reflect his sincerity. Gestures and voice should also convey sincerity.

B. Pathos

Appeals to the emotions should be used to reinforce logic; they should not be used as ends in themselves, nor should an excessive amount of emotional material be used. Sincere, appropriate emotional appeals used *in addition to* the logical appeals enhance the persuasiveness of the speech. Use of emotional appeals designed to "short-circuit" reason, use of emotional appeals without logic, and use of synthetic and superficial emotional appeals will undermine *pathos.* An effective speaker should consider the ways in which the basic needs of his audience, point of view, audience background, and unethical emotional appeals may influence his persuasion.

1. Basic Needs and Emotions. An effective speaker takes into account such psychological needs of his audience as their desire to be respected, to be liked, and to have freedom. If the members of your audience feel that what you are trying to convince them to believe or motivate them to do is desirable and will achieve certain basic drives, you are appealing to their emotions. Speakers often appeal to such emotions as fear, pride, sympathy, pity, and reverence, which are aroused by word pictures, personal examples, illustrations, and descriptions. By means of these details, you create for your audience a vicarious experience in which they "see" what you have seen and "feel" what you have felt.

2. Point of View. Emotional appeals can be presented from different points of view. A scene can be described as if you saw it happen—first-person observation; as if someone else saw it happen—a third-person narrative; or as if it happened to you—first-person narrative. An audience is usually impressed with a firsthand account. For example, if you have seen a starving child stand in line for a meager portion of food, you have a firsthand observation more impressive than a quotation from a congressman who made a one-hour stop in a poverty area. If you have experienced extreme hunger yourself, then a personal account of the sensory aspects of hunger will probably have still greater emotional appeal. Because sincerity is important to persuasion, it is unwise to fictionalize in a speech to persuade.

3. Audience Background. Knowing something about the background of the audience will help you select appeals to use. If you know that all members of your audience are students, you can visualize experiences that all students have had in common. By describing personal events comparable to those experienced by your audience, you evoke *pathos* as well as *ethos.*

4. Unethical Emotional Appeals. Emotional appeal is an important part of a persuasive speech. However, emotional appeal has been exploited by unethical speakers. The effective persuasive speaker should make a deliberate attempt to avoid deceptive uses of emotional appeal. The most common deceptive uses involve the propaganda devices termed bandwagon, card stacking, glittering generality, name calling, plain folks, testimonial, and transfer.

a. Bandwagon. Politicians often use the expression "Hop on the bandwagon," the "everyone-is-doing-it" appeal. They thereby give the impression, correct or not, that the individual is a nonconformist or an outsider if he does not agree with, or do, what they suggest. The listener is made to feel that his sense of belonging is at stake if he fails to think or act as the speaker prescribes.

b. Card Stacking. Card stacking involves the accumulation of deceptive evidence. Ignoring vital but contradictory information, quoting out of context, presenting half-truths, and falsifying testimony are techniques of card stacking. For example, a book reviewer's comment "If you want to read a good book, don't bother to read this one" was subsequently quoted in a speech: "If you want to read a good book, read this one." Investors persuaded by a company's financial reports from only good years will be misled.

c. Glittering Generality. Words with favorable connotations can mislead an audience to uncritical acceptance. A listener may be lulled into accepting a candidate who is "the essence of public spirit." Such expressions as "public spirit," "justice," "glorious birthright," "progressive" are sometimes called "virtue words," because of their power to evoke acceptance or approval without critical thought.

d. Name Calling. When a person or an idea is labeled with an undesirable name, the listener may be led to condemn without careful analysis. Such names as "far left," "new left," "far right," "radicals," "anarchists," and "radical liberals" mean nothing unless these terms are defined.

e. Plain Folks. The "plain folks" device is designed to bridge educational, professional, economic, social, or political gaps. During election periods politicians who visit with their constituents imply that they are "one of the home folks." This is a device of association; the speaker desires to show a pretentious association with individuals whom he wants to exploit.

f. Testimonial. A testimonial is an individual's endorsement of an idea or proposal. For the most part, testimonials are solicited, paid endorsements. If the person making the testimonial is well known or respected in some field, his endorsement may seem less questionable.

g. Transfer. By associating highly respected institutions or symbols with ideas or actions, a speaker may attempt to distract his listener's ability to think critically. Politicians often refer to the expression "as sacred as God, the flag, motherhood, and apple pie" and often use the technique of transfer in reference to these things "held dear by all good Americans." Transfer is sometimes used as a physical device; for example, a politician may put a flag in his lapel. These are unethical appeals to the emotions; a good speaker avoids them.

C. Logos

Persuasion by use of logical proof is based on sound reasoning and dependable evidence. A speaker attempting to persuade must first decide on a proposition that puts forth the conviction or course of action to be proved. A persuasive speech, by its very nature, involves controversial issues; it must have at least two sides, two alternatives. Because the act of persuasion requires audience agreement and acceptance, the speaker attempts to create acceptance by putting forth the most logical and most reasonable arguments.

Once you have decided upon a subject and have defined your position on the issue involved, the first step is to state that decision in the form of a proposition, a statement that can be confirmed or denied. This proposition is the statement of belief or course of action that you want your audience to accept. Your proposition should be a clear declarative statement that advocates a single proposal. It must be a statement of fact, value, or policy. In general, statements of fact and value will be concerned with influencing beliefs; proposals of policy will be concerned with motivating the audience.

The second step will be to consider the important issues of the proposition. If you have decided to convince your audience that capital punishment should be abolished, you should then ask yourself "Why?" What are the reasons for abolishing capital punishment? If you find that the major reasons are that capital punishment is not a deterrent to crime, that it is unconstitutional, and that it is immoral, you will ultimately have to put forth evidence and reasoning to logically prove these issues to your audience. You will find that some issues are self-evident; they will be accepted by your audience with little or no proof. You should try to determine exactly what are the points of agreement and disagreement between your audience and yourself. For example, some audiences might accept the fact that the Bible says "Thou shalt not kill"; no further evidence would be needed. However, it will take more conclusive evidence to prove that capital punishment is not a deterrent to crime. There are statistics and examples available to prove both sides of the argument. Your next step then is to search out the best evidence and to use the most valid forms of reasoning; thus, you can attempt to prove your proposition by logic.

Evidence, the basis of proof, consists mainly of facts and acceptable testimony. Evidence used in the process of induction and deduction brings about logical proof.

1. Inductive Arguments. Induction, from the Latin *inducere*, "to lead into," is the process of examining specific examples within the same category or class and arriving at a conclusion or generalization about the entire category or class; or it is the process or using similar facts, characteristics, or circumstances to argue by analogy.

a. Induction by Example. The precept "Experience is the best teacher" is based on the process of induction by example. A young child soon learns that when he touches the flame of a fire it hurts his finger. A husband concludes that life is much more pleasant when he remembers his wife's birthdays and their anniversaries than when he forgets. A perfect induction occurs when every example within a category or a class is examined. However, it is often impossible or impractical to examine every member of the class involved. Therefore, if an examination of a reasonable number of items indicates that all of the items are identical in some way or that what is true of one item is true of all the items examined, we arrive at a generalization that can be made about *all* of the items within that category: those examined, those not examined, and any that may be examined in the future. If an automobile manufacturer finds that one automobile is incorrectly assembled, other automobiles in that same series will be checked. If the same fault is found in all or even most of the others checked, it is assumed that all of the automobiles in that series may be faulty, and all are called in: those already sold and those waiting to be sold in dealers' showrooms. If you are attempting to prove that capital punishment is not a deterrent to crime, you might very well investigate the states that have abolished capital punishment. If every state that has abolished capital punishment shows no increase in crime following abolishment, you can inductively reason that capital punishment is indeed not a deterrent.

Because most inductive reasoning does not produce an absolute truth or a law, but only a probability, the conclusion is at times discredited or dismissed by the charge that it is merely a generalization. Such a charge may be valid if the speaker has made a hasty generalization or has misunderstood causal relationships. If the speaker remembers the following five rules of induction, his generalizations will be sound.

The examples used must be representative. That is, exceptional or atypical examples must be avoided; only truly representative examples may be used.

The examples used must be current, or at least some current examples must be included. Something that was true in the past is not necessarily still true. However, by using examples from both the past and the present, the speaker can show that an event or trend occurred in the past and is occurring now; he can then reason that it will continue to occur in the future unless something is done.

A sufficient number of examples must be examined. A sufficient number might be defined as enough to assure the audience that the speaker has presented a *fair* amount, enough to discredit a charge of accidental occurrence. At times, one outstanding example will prove a point. However, the probability grows stronger and sounder as the number of instances increases.

An attempt should be made to verify results. If possible, results should be checked with those of others. If a speaker can point out that there is authoritative precedent for his conclusion, it is much more convincing.

If there are exceptions to a speaker's inductive conclusion, he must explain their presence or show that they are inconsequential or infrequent. If contradictory evidence is ignored or suppressed, a knowing audience will refuse to believe other generalizations that the speaker makes.

b. Induction by Analogy. Induction by analogy is the process of arriving at conclusions by comparing similarities. When you observe that two situations, problems, or items are similar in some ways, you can reason that they are *probably* similar in still other ways. Some people reason that because the United Nations is in many ways similar to the League of Nations, it is doomed to failure. What they fail to take into consideration is the fact that there are many differences between the United Nations and the League of Nations. If properly used, however, analogy can have great persuasive power. For effective analogy, the following three rules should be observed.

The points of similarity must be firmly established. Simply saying that two items are similar does not establish them as such. The similarities must clearly show that there is a basis for comparison. If two educational systems have four-year high schools in which comparable courses use similar material, in which the faculties have at least master's degrees and two years of experience, and in which the students made comparable scores on college entrance exams, a reasonable assumption is that the quality of instruction in the high schools is about the same.

The similarities must be pertinent. The similarities must be important similarities, not superficial resemblances. The efficiency of two police forces cannot be compared simply because the men on both forces wear uniforms and badges and carry guns.

The dissimilarities must be explained. Dissimilarities must be shown to be few in number and/or irrelevant. For example, the present stock market is regulated by federal guidelines and safeguards; therefore, it cannot be compared to the stock market of a period prior to federal regulations unless the regulations can be shown to be ineffective.

Although the analogy is one of the most commonly used arguments in everyday speech, it does not establish proof. An analogy simply attempts to establish probability. The degree of probability increases with the number of points of similarity. An analogy has greater power for persuasion if it is used with one of the more logical forms of reasoning. An analogy which attempts to show probability is concerned with examples in the same class. Thus, two educational systems can be compared and two police forces can be compared, but an educational system cannot be compared with a political system and a police force cannot be compared with a fire department.

There is a second kind of analogy, the figurative analogy; it is a rhetorical device designed not to show probability but to help the listener conceive a mental picture or to understand by means of comparison. This analogy involves subjects that are not in the same class. For example, the increase and decrease of tariffs has been compared to turning a faucet on and off. Organized crime with its many branches is often compared to a huge octopus with its many tentacles. A figurative analogy is a stylistic device rather than a logical device. Although a figurative analogy actually proves nothing, it often helps to illustrate ratio, size, or function.

2. *Deductive Arguments.* Deduction, from the Latin *deducere*, meaning "to lead from," is the process of reasoning from a generalization to a conclusion. "Mary is an intelligent girl; she is on the dean's list" and "Bill must have raised his grade average; he is now out for football" are examples of deductive reasoning used to arrive at a conclusion. The reasoning progresses from the generalizations that all students on the dean's list are intelligent, and that all football players must have a certain grade-point average, to specific conclusions concerning Mary and Bill. The reasoning progresses through a three-step procedure called a syllogism: the generalization, termed the major premise; the specific example, termed the minor premise; and the conclusion. The major premise, arrived at by means of an earlier induction, either is known to be true or is assumed to be true. A syllogism takes the following form:

Major premise	All students on the dean's list are intelligent.
Minor premise	Mary is on the dean's list.
Conclusion	Mary is intelligent.

In rhetoric, the process of deduction frequently leaves one of the steps of the syllogism for the audience to complete. Deduction from which one of the three steps has been omitted is called an *enthymeme;* the missing step is completed "in the mind" of the listener. For example, the following syllogism

All teachers in favor of the honor system are idealists.
Dr. Smith is in favor of the honor system.
Therefore, Dr. Smith is an idealist.

might appear in a persuasive speech "Dr. Smith must be an idealist, for he is in favor of the honor system." Enthymemes are the most common form of deductive reasoning to appear in persuasive speeches.

Whether the syllogism is given in complete form or in the form of an enthymeme, the speaker must make certain that his reasoning follows certain rules for deduction. He must also choose the form that best presents his deduction in a persuasive speech.

a. Rules for Deduction. The major premise of a categorical syllogism is a generalization about an entire class; the minor premise refers to a member of that class; and the conclusion follows logically. The rhetorical deduction becomes reliable or certain if (1) the premises are true and (2) the inferences are valid.

The deduction should be based on a generalization that is accepted as a truth as far as common knowledge is concerned. Because the generalization is derived from induction, the checks for induction are also checks for generalization. The minor premise must concern a member of the class mentioned in the generalization, and the generalization must be an accepted truth.

If the syllogism is properly formed, the inferences will be valid. A syllogism must consist of only three terms, with two terms (connected by a verb) present in each of the three statements. Using numbers to designate terms, a syllogism should look like this:

(1) (2)
All *students on the dean's list* are *intelligent.*

(3) (1)
Mary is *on the dean's list.*

(3) (2)
Mary is *intelligent.*

Each term is used twice and must mean the same thing each time it is used. Term 1 is called the middle term of a syllogism and must appear in both the major and minor premises but not in the conclusion. In addition, the major premise must make a positive or negative statement about the *entire class.* Both premises cannot be negative; but if either premise is negative, the conclusion must also be negative. No term can be used in the conclusion that has not been used in the premises.

If the above rules are followed, the conclusion should follow logically from the premises. However, errors in reasoning do occur, either because of poorly worded premises or because of misrepresentation of the major premise. The wording of the major premise must be an acceptable generalization about the entire class and must contain no ambiguous terms. The minor premise must be restricted to a member of the class mentioned in the generalization and must end with the same term that begins the major premise. The following syllogism is invalid because of form.

All criminals oppose legal restrictions.
He opposes legal restrictions.
He is a criminal.

To say that all criminals oppose legal restrictions does not mean that all who oppose legal restrictions are criminals. This is the most common error in deductive reasoning. Note that the minor premise does not end with the same term that begins the major premise. Sharing only one quality with a class does not make an individual a member of that class.

b. Putting Deduction to Work. Although we seldom use the form or language of a syllogism either in conversation or in a speech, we frequently use deductive reasoning in the following six ways.

We may state a generalization and offer proof. For example, we may make the generalization that any nation that suppresses its people is inviting a revolution. We may then offer such proof as mentioning the historical examples of the revolution in France, the many revolutions in South America, and the more recent revolutions in Africa. We would then complete the syllogism by stating that a specific country is now suppressing its people and conclude that the country will soon suffer a revolution.

A generalization may be made and allowed to stand without proof because it is accepted as truth. For example, the statement that organized crime is a threat to every law-abiding citizen does not need a minor premise and a conclusion because no one would argue with the fact that organized crime is a danger to us all.

A speaker may imply the major premise by stating the minor premise and the conclusion. When he makes the statement that John was expelled because he cheated on an exam, he implies that a school rule (a generalization) states that a student cheating on an examination is subject to expulsion.

Only the generalization and the conclusion may be given and the minor premise implied. If a speaker says that only a man who represents the entire school body should be elected senator and follows this with a plea to vote for John Jones for senator, he implies that John Jones will represent the entire school body.

A speaker may state the generalization and the minor premise and imply the conclusion. By stating that all good cheer leaders are fine dancers and that Helen is an outstanding cheer leader, he implies that Helen is also a fine dancer.

Finally, the major premise may adequately imply both the minor premise and the conclusion, although neither is stated. A statement that someone would vote only for a Republican candidate (or a Democratic candidate) implies that anyone else would not get his vote and therefore should not attempt to persuade him to vote any other way.

3. *Evidence.* Once you have established that at least some of your issues must be proved, you must attempt to find evidence to prove them. Evidence consists of the facts used to support your side of an issue. To prove that capital punishment is not a deterrent to crime, you must locate specific statistics and authoritative statements that substantiate what you are trying to prove. Facts are the basis for all induction and deduction.

a. Statistics. Statistics are numerical facts. When you search for the number of crimes that were committed before capital punishment was abolished in a given state and compare it to the number of crimes committed after abolishment in the same state, you have statistics. There are several bases for evaluating statistics.

Are the statistics timely? Your audience will want statistics that bear upon the issue. In general, statistics must be recent to be relevant. However, persuasion involving a survey of a process over several years may use historical as well as current statistics. Use the very latest statistics practical for the issue.

Are the statistics fair and accurate? Try to use statistics that are as unbiased as possible. Television stations are known to "load" their programming during the period that ratings are made. Politicians are known to quote opinion polls that show they are winning when opponents quote polls showing just the opposite. Evaluate the source of statistics and make the source clear to your audience, who will also be concerned about reliability.

Are the statistics relevant? You should find out exactly what the figures used refer to. In advertising, such expressions as "Nine out of ten doctors recommend . . ." are often used. You should determine what *kinds* of doctors are doing the recommending. Are they M.D.s (which is implied), Ph.D.s, dentists, or veterinarians? Are they doctors in private practice, doctors employed by the institution or company making the statement, new doctors, interns? Unless you know exactly what the figures mean, they may not be relevant to what you are attempting to prove. Also beware of averages, which may have little significance. (Many have drowned in a stream that *averaged* three feet in depth.)

Are the statistics logical? Many people will take statistics at face value simply because they are statistics. Typographical errors do occur and memories do fade. Check your statistics against other statistics or facts. Be careful of statistics that do not sound logical. If you find that something fails to "ring true," be certain to question it before you use it.

b. Authority. An authority may be an individual or a printed source. In certain circumstances an individual may be an authority simply because he was there at the time; he was a witness. In most cases, however, an authority is a person who is an expert in a particular field. If the authority is a printed source, such as an encyclopedia or a dictionary, the following questions should be asked:

Is the source a primary (original) one? If not, does it quote the primary source accurately? Is the source used the original printing or a reissue?

Is the source a recent one? In most cases the latest edition or issue should be used.

Is the source unbiased? Publications, even prestige publications, are known to be biased on certain issues. As far as possible, try to use sources that are acknowledged to be unbiased.

If the authority is an individual, the following questions should be asked:

Is the individual qualified physically, mentally, and morally? Does he have any physical limitations that may invalidate the opinion expressed? Does the individual have normal or better than average intelligence? Can the integrity of the individual be assured?

Is the individual an authority? If he is an authority, is he an authority in the area under consideration? Well-meaning authorities may venture comments in areas about which they are relatively uninformed. An outstanding authority in one field is not an authority in every field. However, many individuals are authorities in more than one field, particularly in related fields. Has the individual had sufficient opportunity to know the facts about which he speaks?

Is the individual prejudiced? This question must be carefully considered, for all human beings tend to have prejudice in areas. This is particularly true if one is involved financially, occupationally, or socially with the situation he is discussing, or if he has family ties or organizational affiliation. What reason may the source have to distort the facts, present only one side, or slant the information?

Is too much reliance placed upon one source? It is often advisable to consult several reliable sources. This principle is illustrated nobly in the case of physicians who call other physicians for consultation about a diagnosis. Use of a single source bespeaks inadequate preparation or reliance on a minority source. An impressive case is founded on the opinions of several reliable sources.

Is the source substantiated? An opinion should appear to be sound in the light of the facts upon which it bears, and in the light of reason. Expert opinion always seems strong if it is supported by statistics or other facts.

The speech to persuade sets forth a proposition; the proposition, in turn, must be presented to the audience as a series of issues. The issues themselves are subject to proof in the form of induction and deduction. The materials of proof are statistics and authoritative statements; in other words, the evidence. Further progress of the speech to persuade depends upon the purpose of the speech: the speaker will attempt either to influence the convictions or beliefs of his audience in a speech to convince, or to influence the actions or behavior of his audience in a speech to motivate.

II. THE SPEECH TO CONVINCE

A speaker who attempts to persuade his audience to acknowledge that his proposition is factual or that it has value is attempting to convince. He is trying to influence thought but not action. The speaker's persuasion is directed to gaining acceptance or approval of his belief. He presents his issues and defends them with facts and logic. A speaker delivers a speech to convince before an audience that is uninformed, that is impassive, or that is in disagreement with the views held by the speaker.

A. The Subject

A *proposition of fact* expresses the speaker's belief that a condition or situation either exists or does not exist. The speaker may attempt to convince his audience that conditions in the ghettos of our country make them unlivable, that certain public officials are guilty of conflict of interest, or that Communism is a threat to the free world. A *proposition of value* is concerned with a value judgment made by the speaker; it often involves ethical matters. Propositions of value express the speaker's judgment concerning the worth, importance, or justification of something. The speaker may attempt to convince his audience that the United States was justified in entering a particular war, that the American system of secondary education is the best in the world, or that the present welfare system suppresses initiative.

B. The Organization

After the speaker has defined his proposition and analyzed the issues involved, he must determine which ethical appeals, which logical appeals, which illustrations, examples, and proof will best convince his audience.

The introduction must be carefully planned, for it is in this portion of his speech that he must present to his audience the proposition and what he considers to be the issues. In the body of the speech each issue must be stated and proved, so that little or no doubt remains in the minds of the audience. The transitions between the issues must be smooth, and they must keep the issues in a clear perspective. The speaker should maintain unity by showing how each point supports the single purpose of the speech. The conclusion must sustain and reinforce the interest of the audience. The major issues should be repeated, and the speaker should end with a confident restatement of the proposition.

III. THE SPEECH TO MOTIVATE

When the speaker attempts to persuade his audience that they should take a specific course of action, he attempts to motivate. He is asking his audience to act on a specific policy. The speaker points out a definite method for meeting an established need. A careful analysis of the audience will determine how much time must be used for establishing the need. If the audience is entirely friendly, such as a partisan political audience, little or no time may be required for the need arguments and the entire speech can be devoted to the plan of action. However, if the audience is antagonistic, the speaker should not move to his plan of action until the need is established.

A. The Subject

A proposition of policy involves principles, procedures, and conduct. The speaker suggests specific steps to be taken to remedy a situation and attempts to persuade the audience with emotional appeals and with logical appeals to take the recommended action. The action being requested may be something that is needed immediately, such as a strike, or it may be a long-range policy concerned with neighborhood renewal.

B. The Organization

The organization of a speech to motivate is more obvious than that of a speech to convince. Generally, the body of a speech to motivate has three parts. First, if the need is not understood by the audience, then it must be established. If the audience is sympathetic to the need, the need should at least be mentioned. Second, the speaker details how the plan of action will work. Third, the speaker points out how the plan will meet the needs and how it will be practical and beneficial.

As in the speech to convince, the introduction, transitions, proof, and conclusions are all important. The introduction should state the issues, the plan should be clear, the benefits should be established, and the conclusion should again point out how the plan of action will meet the needs and how it will benefit all concerned. If the members of the audience have been persuaded that the suggested course of action is the best one and that all those concerned will benefit from it, they should be motivated to take action.

SUMMARY

The speech to persuade may be a speech to convince or a speech to motivate. In the first type, the speaker is concerned with the convictions or beliefs of his audience; in the second type, he is concerned with their actions. A speaker persuades by a combination of emotional appeals, ethical appeals, and logical appeals.

A speaker's personal persuasion is termed *ethos.* Personal persuasion is based on the speaker's reputation, his appearance, the content of his speech, and his delivery.

A speaker's use of emotional appeal is termed *pathos.* Proper emotional appeals should always be appropriate, should be used only in conjunction with logical appeals, and should be used in moderation. Use of emotional appeal should be based on the needs of the audience, the speaker's point of view, the audience's background, and a knowlege of unethical appeals.

A speaker's use of fact and reasoning is termed *logos.* Because a topic for a persuasive speech is controversial, the speaker must attempt to establish support for his belief by using the best evidence he can find. He should state his belief in the form of a clear proposition, locate the major issues, and support these issues with arguments based on proof. Induction and deduction are the most commonly used methods of proof; both use evidence.

Induction proceeds from the examination of specific items within a class to a generalization about that class. Most induction is based on induction by examples, which must be representative, current, sufficient in number, and verified by other sources; any contradictory evidence must be explained. A second kind of induction is analogy, which does not prove but which shows probability. If the speaker shows that two situations, problems, or items are similar in some important ways, he can conclude that they are similar in other ways. The points of similarity must be firmly established and pertinent, and any dissimilarities must be explained.

Deduction is the process of reasoning from a generalization to a conclusion. The process, known as a syllogism, consists of three parts: the major premise, the minor premise, and the conclusion. A rhetorical deduction is considered reliable if the premises are true and the inferences are valid. To be valid, a syllogism must be properly formed.

Evidence consists of facts, either statistics or authoritative statements. The statistics used should be pertinent, fair and accurate, relative, and logical. Statements by authority are of two kinds: written authority and individual authority. The written authority should be a primary source, as recent as possible, and as unbiased as possible. The individual should be qualified physically, mentally, and morally; he should be an established authority; he should be unprejudiced; and he should be supported by other sources.

Use of ethical proof, emotional proof, and logical proof to persuade an audience that a proposition is either factual or has value is speaking to convince. Use of the three types of proof to persuade an audience to take a specific course of action is speaking to motivate.

ASSIGNMENTS

For the following speeches prepare an outline and present the outline to your instructor just prior to your speaking.

1. Prepare a speech based on a proposition of fact (see page 110). You are to convince your audience that a condition or a situation exists or does not exist. Your outline should consist of from two to five points that are issues for supporting your contention. Be certain that your subpoints support the issues and that each is adequately proved. Time: 6-10 minutes.
2. Prepare a speech based on a proposition of value (see page 110). You are to convince your audience that something is or is not worthwhile, important, or justified. Your outline should consist of from two to five major points that are issues for supporting your contention. Be certain that your subpoints support the issues and that each is adequately proved. Time: 6-10 minutes.
3. Prepare a speech to motivate. You are to persuade your audience that they should take a specific course of action. You may find that you must present need arguments as part of your speech or that you can concentrate on persuading the audience that your plan of action is beneficial and practical. Time: 6-10 minutes.

chapter ten

DISCUSSION

Discussion, carried on for the purpose of acquiring information or reaching a decision, occurs at all levels of communication from councils and cabinets to communes and classrooms. It is carried on in the United Nations, in Congress, in state legislatures, in city councils, and in the classroom—any place where facts, values, and policies are determined. According to the situation, the type of discussion varies in formality from an informal classroom discussion to a formal lecture forum.

Effective participation in discussion requires both knowledge and skill. A discussion participant should know how to phrase a discussion question, how to classify the purpose of a discussion, how to prepare for a discussion, how to participate in a discussion, and how to lead the various types of discussions.

I. PHRASING THE QUESTION

A discussion topic must be phrased as a question. The question should exhibit pertinency, fairness, clarity, limitation, and appropriateness.

The topic must be worded as a question. One of the basic differences between debate and discussion is the wording of the topic. In a debate concerned with the problem of population growth, the proposition would be worded as a declarative statement: The United States government should limit the size of families. For discussion the form is that of a question: "What should the United States do about its population problem?"

The topic should be pertinent. The best sources for ideas for discussion questions are the latest newspapers and magazines. Find out what is being discussed throughout the country and around the world. It is much more interesting to discuss a topic that is currently important.

The topic should be worded fairly. The discussion question should be worded impartially, so that it does not show a bias for a particular point of view. The question "Should the dangerous game of football be abolished?" suggests a judgment before the group even begins discussion.

The topic should be worded clearly. The question should avoid abstract words. The question "Should untrustworthy government officials be penalized?" is not clear. Questions will immediately be asked concerning such unclear terms as "untrustworthy" and "penalized." A better question might be "Should government officials who are members of the communist party be dismissed?" As far as possible, the questions should be stated in clear and simple terms that are easily understood.

The topic should be limited. Double subjects and comparisons should be avoided. Questions such as "Should the federal government or state government solve the pollution problem?" or "Should football replace baseball as our national pastime?" are not good questions because they probably cannot be discussed in the time allotted and because they are somewhat ambiguous. The question "What can be done to stop wars?" is obviously too broad and could not be adequately covered. A better question would be "What can the United Nations do to stop wars?" Proper limitation of the questions will improve the quality of the discussion and avoid inadequate coverage of the subject. The topic should be important enough to be easily discussed, yet simple enough to be manageable.

The topic should be appropriate. Those participating in a discussion should feel not only that the topic is appropriate for them to be discussing but also that their discussion of the topic may bring about some ultimate influence. If the members of the group or members of the audience are convinced that they should do something after hearing the discussion, and they find that they can do nothing, frustration occurs. For example, discussing a question such as "What should be the foreign policy of China?" would be useless because members of the group have no influence; however, a discussion of the question "Should our school abolish letter grades?" might actually influence the school's administration.

II. CLASSIFYING THE PURPOSE

Many types of problems are considered for discussion. However, they tend to fall into three categories: problems of fact, problems of value, and problems of policy.

All three types of discussion questions must be based on facts. Intelligent discussion cannot take place without knowledge. A sharing of personal opinions not based on research can at best result in only a short discussion, limited in both scope and value.

A. Problems of Fact

Problems of fact are usually involved with interpretation and prediction: "Do the Russians plan to dominate the world?" "Will France continue as a world power?" "Will the British monetary system withstand outside pressures?" Answers to such questions as these, although involved with facts, can only be surmised. Such topics as "Does use of the honor system during examinations work?" "Is the crime rate increasing faster than population growth?" "Does television contribute to juvenile delinquency?" are concerned with interpretation. Questions which can be answered with common knowledge or with simple "yes" or "no" are not suitable for discussion.

B. Problems of Value

Problems of value relate to standards of taste as well as to levels of influence. "How important is it to attend college?" "How influential is personal appearance to social behavior?" "How beneficial is modern art?" Problems of value are resolved in judgments formed from known facts and opinions.

C. Problems of Policy

Problems of policy are worded so that they request a specific course of action after an evaluation of various alternatives. "How should the federal government conserve our natural resources?" "What should be the college's policy concerning attendance?" "What should the federal government do about inflation?" Questions of fact and value often arise during the course of a discussion of policy.

III. PREPARING FOR DISCUSSION

An interesting and productive discussion requires planning and preparation. Each participant should prepare an analytical outline, gather information, and prepare a discussion outline.

A. The Analytical Outline

An analytical outline for discussion begins with an expansion of the idea that a problem exists. In five basic steps, a discussion group must (1) recognize the existence of a problem; (2) locate, define, and limit the problem; (3) explore solutions to the problem and determine standards for use in evaluating the solutions; (4) develop and evaluate the various solutions to the problems and determine which solution is the most effective; (5) examine ways and means of putting the solution into practice, a step that also results in the testing of the soundness of the solution.

An analytical outline consists of a series of questions concerning these five steps. Following is an example of an analytical outline for discussion.

What should be the role of government in regulating organized labor?

I. Definition and limitation of the problem
  A. What do the terms mean?
    1. What does "role" mean in this context?
    2. How should "government" be defined?
      a. National or federal governments?
      b. State and/or local governments?
    3. What does the term "regulating" mean?
    4. How can "organized labor" be defined?
    5. Are there other terms which need to be defined at this time?
  B. Can or should the problem be limited in any way for purposes of discussion?

II. Analysis of the problem
  A. Historically, what has been the role of government in regulating organized labor?
    1. What was the "doctrine of conspiracy"?
    2. What was the attitude of government with respect to the formation of national labor unions?
      a. National Labor Union?
      b. Knights of Labor?
      c. American Federation of Labor?
    3. How did federal legislation affect union activities?
      a. Sherman Act?

b. Clayton Act?
c. Norris-LaGuardia Act?
4. What was the attitude of the New Deal toward organized labor?
a. As expressed in the NIRA?
b. As expressed in the Wagner Act?
c. As expressed in the Fair Labor Standards Act?
5. What explains the postwar reaction against labor as expressed in the Taft-Hartley Act?

B. What is the present attitude of government with respect to the regulation of organized labor?
1. What is the attitude of national government?
a. What are the provisions of the Taft-Hartley Act?
b. What are the provisions of the Landrum-Griffin Act?
2. What is the attitude of state governments?
a. "Right-to-work" laws?
b. State labor relations boards?

C. Are there any indications of a need to regulate the activities of organized labor?
1. What are the causes of concern with activities of organized labor?
a. Union security agreements?
b. Charges of "corrupt leadership"?
c. Handling of welfare funds?
d. Coercive activities?
e. "Racketeering"?
f. Political activities of unions?
2. Are the activities of organized labor in harmony with the best interests of our society?

D. What are the effects of present labor activities?
1. What is the attitude of the general public toward labor?
2. What is the attitude of management?
3. What is the attitude of the individual worker?
4. What is the attitude of organized labor?
5. How do these attitudes affect collective bargaining?

III. Statement of criteria

A. What goals are we seeking to achieve in government regulation of organized labor?
1. What are the economic goals?
2. What are the political goals?
3. What are the social goals?

B. What other objectives are desirable?
1. Should we increase the bargaining power of unions?
2. Should we increase the bargaining power of management?
3. Should the general welfare be paramount to the interests of either labor or management?

C. Are there other goals or objectives?

IV. Possible solutions
   A. Should the national government take a more active or less active role in regulating the activities of organized labor?
      1. In what areas?
      2. By what methods?
   B. Should the state governments take a more active or less active role in regulating the activities of organized labor?
      1. In what areas?
      2. By what methods?
   C. Should present laws and regulations be made more adequate to cope with the existing situation?
   D. Are there any additional possible solutions?

V. Evaluation of solutions
   A. What would be the consequences of following each projected course of action?
   B. How and to what extent would each of the proposed solutions deal with the causes of the problem?
   C. In what way and to what extent would each proposed solution meet the goals and objectives previously established?
   D. What are the advantages of each proposed solution?
   E. Are there any disadvantages to proposed courses of action?

VI. Most desirable solution (What appears to be the best solution?)

VII. Application
   A. What steps should be taken to put this solution into operation?
      1. By what methods?
      2. By whom?
   B. What obstacles are likely to be encountered?

A satisfactory analytical outline can be written for any problem simply by using general knowledge. Some groups achieve a better analytical outline by working as a group rather than working individually. In any case, an analytical outline should act as a guide during the second step, the gathering of information.

B. Gathering Information

As a discussion participant you must be certain that you can answer the questions on the analytical outline. As you gather information, you should be able to enlarge upon the analytical outline. Throughout the process of gathering information, make certain that your information is accurate and your sources reliable.

1. Discussion Cards. Record information from books and magazines on 4″ x 6″ cards, which are easy to organize and handle before and during the discussion. Figure 8 shows an example of a discussion card.

Corrupt Union Leadership II., C., 1., b.

Howard Jones, Prof. of Pol. Sci., Newsweek, Jan. 16, 1971.

A great number of the leaders of the larger labor unions either have criminal records or are known to have strong ties with known criminals.

p. 35

Figure 8. Discussion Card.

The card should have a title, or subject, or heading of as few words as possible. This title, placed at the top left corner of the card, should tell at a glance what the entire quotation is about. The source information, placed two or three spaces below the subject, can be called the four "Ws": *w*ho said it, *w*hat makes him an authority, *w*here can it be found in writing, and *w*hen was it published? The quotation, placed two or three spaces below the source information, needs no quotation marks. It should contain a single idea. The page number is placed in the lower right corner of the card. For easy use, the card can be indexed to correspond to the outline. Note that this information, placed at the top right corner of the card, documents point II., C., 1., b. of the analytical outline. It should be made in pencil because it may change position between the analytical outline and the discussion outline.

2. *Testing Evidence.* Evidence is information that furnishes any type of proof. Tests of evidence fall into two divisions: tests of facts and tests of opinion. (See Chapter 9, where such tests are explained.)

C. The Discussion Outline

The discussion outline is quite similar to the analytical outline. The major difference is that, rather than using questions for the outline, you use the answers that you now have. To answer the question "What does 'role' mean in this context?" (I., A., 1.) you have *at least* one discussion card defining the term. A second difference is the fact that the discussion outline is usually much longer and more involved than the analytical outline. During the process of gathering information, ideas, history, criteria, and solutions not covered in the analytical outline are brought to light. These should be incorporated into the discussion outline.

IV. PARTICIPATION

A discussion is the *cooperative* effort of individuals attempting to arrive at a solution that is acceptable to the entire group. Individuals should work for group unity, participate actively, and speak effectively.

A. Group Unity

The object of the discussion group is to find an answer to a problem. This can best be achieved if the group works as a unit rather than individually. Speakers who discuss together should have some knowledge of the background and personalities of other members of the group. If possible, the speakers should get together to compile the analytical outline; this meeting is an excellent time for them to get acquainted. If a meeting before the discussion is not possible, then the chairman should have the speakers meet off stage, where he can make introductions in which he gives pertinent information about the background of the participants. He is really a social and public-relations director at this point. It is of great importance that the speakers be made to feel comfortable in the discussion situation, for only then can they speak freely and sincerely. Actually, most speakers in a discussion find that they speak more easily than in individual speaking situations. The fact that everyone in the discussion group shares the responsibility of presenting the proposition tends to decrease apprehension; at the same time, it stimulates thought. During the discussion, unity is possible only if each member of the group is objective, tolerant, and unemotional.

Be objective. Make every attempt to be impartial and open-minded in your views. Every view and opinion should be heard and weighed against the evidence presented. Consider an idea on its merits alone; do not project personal views or prejudices.

Be tolerant. Be tolerant of opposing views; keep in mind that a discussion actually accomplishes nothing if there is total agreement at the onset.

Be unemotional. Although interest, expectancy, and enthusiasm are often at a high pitch during discussion, they must not hinder your concentration on facts and sound thinking.

B. Active Participation

Each member of the discussion group should contribute, listen carefully, and take notes.

Contribute. The information you have may change the collective mind of the group. If you have contradictory evidence, present it. Only by knowing *all* of the facts can the group make a wise decision. In all fairness to other members of the group, participate but do not monopolize discussion time.

Listen. Rather than listening to what is being said, a discussion member who is disorganized and poorly prepared often reads over his own material or tries to locate something that he believes he has read. Such an individual too often disrupts a discussion by asking unnecessary questions.

Take notes. Not only should you listen carefully to what is being said; you should also take careful notes. All members of the discussion group should take notes on the comments of every other member. When the group is ready to discuss the best solution, each member should have the same basic information. Members will not be asked to repeat a statement or figures accurately recorded in note form.

C. Use of Language

An individual participating in a discussion should articulate and pronounce words with care. He should be precise and objective in his use of language.

Be precise. Language used should be precise and exact. If possible, give exact figures and numbers as well as precise quotations. If there can be any question about the meaning of a word or expression, define it. Avoid generalizations and ambiguities.

Be objective. Be as impersonal and unprejudiced as possible in your use of language. Be tactful in what you say. Feel free to disagree but do so in a tactful way. Avoid telling another member of the group that he is all wrong or that what he said is illogical or foolish. You might say instead, "Let us look at another side" or "Have you considered another possible interpretation?" Derogatory words and expressions should also be avoided. Give a constructive emphasis to your comments, for in this way you can direct the discussion toward a more amiable solution.

V. LEADING DISCUSSION

In discussion, someone is usually designated as the leader. He may be either a member of the group or someone outside the group. In either case he is responsible for guiding the members of the group to a satisfactory solution and should be the best informed of the group. The leader is responsible for the preparations, for the introductions, for controlling the discussion, for summarizations, and, if necessary, for guiding audience participation.

A. Preparation

In some cases the leader is responsible for the planning of the entire discussion. It may be his duty to phrase the discussion topic, to ensure the participation of qualified participants, to publicize the discussion, to help with the analytical outline, and to prepare a bibliography.

In addition, the leader is usually responsible for the physical arrangements. He should arrange the seating so that those participating in the discussion can see each other's faces while they talk. If there is an audience present, the participants should be able to see each other *and* the audience. The circle, the semicircle, the square, and the oblong are effective arrangements. If at all possible, the participants should be seated around a table to facilitate their handling of writing materials, outlines, and discussion cards. The discussion leader should be seated at the head of the table or midway in a semicircular arrangement.

B. Introductions

As mentioned, the leader should have pertinent information about the background of the participants. If the members do not know each other, it is the duty of the leader to make introductions. In addition, the leader should introduce the participants to the audience, if there is an audience. He should also give a general introduction including the reasons why the question is being discussed and why it is important. He should conclude his general introduction with a transition into the discussion itself. Part of the transition should be a statement of the discussion topic.

C. Control

The leader should be in control of the discussion at all times. Probably he will give most of his attention to keeping the discussion on the subject and to drawing all members of the group into the discussion. He must tactfully keep those who would monopolize the discussion from doing so and encourage the less aggressive members to contribute to the discussion. The leader should ask "leading" questions to encourage complete discussion of all important points. At times, the leader may be required to settle arguments diplomatically, to help make decisions, and to define the issues.

D. Summaries and Transitions

After a phase of the problem has been sufficiently discussed, the leader should summarize that portion of the discussion and define what agreement was reached, and make a transition to the following phase. At the conclusion of the discussion, the leader should make a final summary.

E. Guiding Audience Participation

If an audience is present and is expected to participate, the leader is responsible for guiding that participation. Before opening the discussion to questions from the audience, the leader should inform the audience of the proper procedure for asking questions: participants from the audience should gain recognition from the leader, then direct their questions to a single member of the discussion group or indicate that anyone can answer it. The leader should make certain that no single member of the audience is allowed to dominate the question period.

The leader should repeat each question asked by a member of the audience. At times, he may feel that for clarification it is necessary to reword the question. He may also find that because of the way the question is worded or because of the type of question, he may have to diplomatically refuse to direct the question to the group.

V. TYPES OF DISCUSSION

The many social situations in which people find themselves have caused the development of a variety of discussion patterns. The patterns fall into two divisions: informal (or closed) discussions and formal (or open) discussions.

A. Informal Discussions

Informal, or closed, discussion is discussion in which the participants follow a planned procedure but are involved in solving a problem or making a decision for their own benefit, not for the benefit of a listening audience. Informal discussions fall into four types: class discussions, round-table discussions, business meetings, and committee meetings.

1. Class Discussions. Teachers often use the discussion method to make teaching more interesting. With the teacher acting as leader, the entire class participates. Facts, opinions, and ideas are expressed by the students in answer to the leading questions asked by the teacher or other students.

2. Round-Table Discussions. The participants in a round-table discussion are seated in a circle. The circle contributes to unity, friendliness, cooperation, and freedom. It is often used by professional people to discuss specific problems in an informal way.

3. Business Meetings. Business meetings take place when an organization considers the affairs of the group concerned. Each matter for consideration is adequately discussed. Usually, more than one problem is discussed during a business meeting, with the chairman or an officer of the organization leading the discussion according to the plan of an agenda.

4. Committee Meetings. Committees are usually appointed to investigate or act. Such a committee should be composed of people having a variety of points of view. Problems are usually solved more easily and efficiently in a committee meeting than in a meeting of the entire group.

B. Formal Discussions

Formal or open discussion is discussion in which the participants are actually directing the information toward the audience. Formal discussion involves four types: panel discussions, symposium discussions, lecture forums, and dialogue.

1. Panel Discussions. A panel consists of a small group conversing together in the presence of a larger group (or a judge). The panel should consist of four to eight persons and a chairman, seated in a semicircle and facing the audience. The time devoted to a panel discussion program is often controlled; for example, it may be a one-hour program made up roughly of forty minutes of panel discussion and twenty minutes of discussion from the audience.

Although a panel discussion is sometimes rehearsed, a rehearsal may preclude the enthusiasm and spontaneity of an unrehearsed discussion.

2. *Symposium Discussions.* The symposium differs from the panel discussion in that the symposium members are authorities on a topic or question and each member presents a prepared talk on one important phase of the problem. The symposium, which usually consists of two or four participants and a chairman or leader, imposes time limits for each of the speeches. The purpose of the symposium is to provide the audience with a set of speeches which explore a subject from several significant points of view.

The chairman in a symposium discussion does not need the extensive preparation that he needs for a panel discussion. However, he announces the subject for discussion, introduces the speakers to the audience, presides during the symposium, relates the speeches to each other, summarizes, and presides during the audience participation. The chairman may introduce all of the speakers at the beginning of the program or he may introduce each speaker as he gives his speech. Each introduction should help the audience to understand and appreciate the qualifications of each expert. The chairman must listen carefully so that he can summarize properly and relate the speeches to each other. Furthermore, the chairman serves as a timekeeper and sees that the speakers observe the time limits.

The symposium speakers selected should be excellent authorities on the topic they discuss, and each one should be assigned an important phase of the topic, which differs from the phases discussed by other speakers. Each of the speakers should relate his speech to the speeches of the others. A speaker may also use as much as a third of his time adapting his remarks to those of the preceding speakers. If one speaker differs with the other speakers, he should show respect for, and appreciation of, the other speakers' point of view.

Questions may or may not be asked of the participants. If the audience participates, the symposium becomes a symposium forum.

3. *Lecture Forums.* The lecture forum consists of a chairman and a lecturer, whose address is followed by a discussion period. The chairman announces the topic and introduces the lecturer. The chairman also presides during the forum period.

The speaker should be an authority on the lecture topic. In some cases, a group may invite a lecturer to speak to them on a phase of a subject about which they wish to secure additional information.

4. *The Dialogue.* The dialogue is a form of discussion in which one person questions a second person. The person being questioned

should be an expert in some field. However, the individual asking the questions must also be well informed. The person asking the questions also serves as chairman.

The questioner should ask questions that the audience would like to have answered. He should take pains to ask questions whose answers will give the audience comprehensive and accurate knowledge about the subject discussed. If possible, the chairman should consult with the guest in connection with planning the program; however, the questions and answers should be spontaneous.

The chairman begins the program by announcing the topic and introducing the respondent. The chairman plans at least some of the questions beforehand and arranges them so that an appropriate thought pattern evolves during the dialogue. Additional questions should occur as the program unfolds. The chairman usually comments on some of the answers. The chairman may summarize the dialogue if he thinks it would be helpful. Following the dialogue, the chairman announces that the program is open to questions and comments from the floor. At the close of the audience-participation period, the chairman summarizes the entire program.

SUMMARY

A discussion topic must be worded as a question which explores a problem of fact, value, or policy.

To prepare for a discussion, each member should prepare an analytical outline that includes questions concerning definitions and limitations of the problem, the analysis of the problem, statements of criteria, possible solutions, evaluations of solutions, the most desirable solution, and application of the best solution. In addition, each member must gather information and record the information on discussion cards. Each member should also apply the tests of evidence. Each member of the discussion group should apply his research to preparation of a discussion outline.

Participation in a discussion should stress group unity: each member should be objective, tolerant, and unemotional; each member should actively participate by contributing, listening attentively, and taking notes.

A discussion leader should introduce the discussion members to each other and to the audience; he should introduce the question, make transitions, and summarize. He should direct the entire discussion, including any audience participation.

Discussion falls into two divisions: informal discussion, which includes class discussion, round-table discussion, business meetings, and committee meetings; and formal discussion, which includes panel discussion, symposium discussion, lecture forum, and dialogue.

ASSIGNMENTS

1. As part of a class discussion, discuss possible topics for panel and symposium discussions. You may want to choose a class chairman and/or secretary. In addition, you may want to appoint committees to search various sources for additional topics.
2. Prepare for panel discussions. The class should be divided into groups of from six to eight people. If class members volunteer for specific discussion topics, each group should select its chairman. If the instructor appoints members to the groups, he should also appoint a chairman for each group. Each group should construct an analytical outline under the guidance of its chairman. Each member of the group should locate information to answer the questions on the analytical outline and prepare an individual discussion outline. Each panel discussion group should take one class period for its presentation. Your outlines as well as your presentation will be graded by the instructor.
3. Prepare for symposium discussion. The class should be divided into groups of two or four. One member of each group should act as chairman for the group. Each member of the group should become an expert on some aspect of the discussion question. If the symposium consists of two members, the pro and con of the question should be presented. If the group consists of four members, each member may discuss an important aspect of the discussion question or two members may discuss the pro and con of the present system and the other two present the pro and con of a proposed solution. Each group should take one class period for its presentation. Present a copy of your outline to your instructor just prior to your speaking.
4. Arrange to have a lecturer or an authority make a presentation to the class. Ask him to speak for fifteen to twenty minutes. Each member of the class should become knowledgeable concerning the topic. Each member of the class should offer questions, upon which his research will be evaluated.
5. The class should be divided into groups of two. One member of the class should be an expert on a topic; the other should engage in a dialogue with the "expert." Each group of two should make a thirty-minute presentation.

appendix
EVALUATION SHEETS

SPEAKER EVALUATION — EMOTIONAL RESPONSE

Speaker ____

Place ________________________________ Time __________

Statements *Emotional Response*

1.

2.

3.

4.

5.

6.

7.

8.

9.

10.

11.

12.

13.

14.

15.

Evaluator ______________________

Class ________________________

SPEAKER EVALUATION — DELIVERY

Speaker ____

Place ______________________________ Time __________

Was the speaker poised or nervous? Give reasons.

Did the speaker have good or bad speaker-audience relationship? Give reasons.

Did the speaker have good or bad posture? Give reasons.

Did the speaker have good or bad gestures and movements? Give reasons.

Did the speaker have vocal variety? Give reasons.

Did the speaker have a pleasing quality? Give reasons.

Did the speaker articulate clearly and pronounce correctly? Give negative examples.

Did the speaker speak at a moderate rate? Too fast or slow? Vocalized pauses?

Evaluator ______________________

Class __________________________

SPEAKER EVALUATION — CONTENT

Speaker ____

Place ______________________________ Time __________

Introduction

Get Attention? How?
Present Topic? How?
Make Transitions? How?

Body

Divisions Mentioned? In what way?
List the major points:

I.
  A.
  B.

II.
  A.
  B.

III.
  A.
  B.

IV.
  A.
  B.

Conclusion

Introduce conclusion? How?
Summarize? In what way?
Make a concluding statement? How?

Evaluator ____________________

Class ______________________

SPEAKER EVALUATION — CONTENT

Speaker ____

Place ____________________________________ Time __________

Subject ____

Issue	*Argument for*	*Argument against*

Issue	*Argument for*	*Argument against*

Issue	*Argument for*	*Argument against*

Issue	*Argument for*	*Argument against*

Issue	*Argument for*	*Argument against*

Evaluator ____________________

Class ________________________

SPEAKER EVALUATION Name ______________ Speech ______________

Directions: Evaluate the speaker in each of the areas indicated by circling one of the numbers from 1 (lowest) to 5 (highest). Grades: 40-45 = A; 35-39 = B; 30-34 = C; 25-29 = D; 0-24 = F.

Test ✓

I. Preparation
  A. Arrangement
    1. Introduction — 1 2 3 4 5
      a. Interesting and attention getting?
      b. General introduction of subject?
      c. Transition into body of speech?
    2. Body — 1 2 3 4 5
      a. Logical organization?
      b. Pertinent material?
      c. Transitions within body?
    3. Outline — 1 2 3 4 5
      a. Major points distinct and clear?
      b. Outline easily understood?
      c. Outline in good form?
    4. Conclusion — 1 2 3 4 5
      a. Summarize?
      b. Conclude?
  B. Material — 1 2 3 4 5
    1. Good choice of subject?
    2. Introduction, body, conclusion related?
    3. Within time limits?

Test

II. Presentation
  A. Mental Process — 1 2 3 4 5
    1. Poised?
    2. Established rapport?
  B. Speaker-audience relationship — 1 2 3 4 5
    1. Good visual contact?
      a. Looked over, under, or away?
      b. Scanned well?
    2. Good ear contact?
  C. Posture, Gestures, Movement — 1 2 3 4 5
    1. Good joint lineup?
    2. Good gestures?
    3. Too much hand movement?
    4. Too much shifting?
  D. Voice — 1 2 3 4 5
    1. Vocal variety?
    2. Moderate rate?
    3. Clear articulation?
    4. Proper pronunciation?
    5. Pleasing quality?

Total Score ______________

Additional Remarks:

DISCUSSION EVALUATION

Group ______ Discussion Question ____________________________

Directions: The elements to consider in your evaluation are analysis, evidence, listening, logical reasoning, adaptation, cooperation, language, delivery, and number of participations. Give reasons for your evaluation. In the space provided, rank each speaker as superior (A), excellent (B), good (C), fair (D), or below average (F).

1. Name ______________________________ Rank __________
Reasons for Evaluation:

2. Name ______________________________ Rank __________
Reasons for Evaluation:

3. Name ______________________________ Rank __________
Reasons for Evaluation:

4. Name ______________________________ Rank __________
Reasons for Evaluation:

5. Name ______________________________ Rank __________
Reasons for Evaluation:

6. Name ______________________________ Rank __________
Reasons for Evaluation:

Evaluator ____________________

Class ________________________

SPEAKER EVALUATION — DEBATE

1st Aff. Speaker ______________ Representing ____________________

Place ____ Time __________

Proposition ____

I. (first major point)

  A. (first supporting argument)

    1. (evidence)

    2.

    3.

  B. (second supporting argument)

    1.

    2.

    3.

II. (second major point)

  A.

    1.

    2.

    3.

  B.

    1.

    2.

    3.

Evaluator ________________________

Class ___________________________

Index

A

B

C

K

L

M

N

O

P

T

U

V

W

Y